MW00334435

Lighter Than Air

My Life in its Time

by

Robert Warren Rose

Page design by Brendan Clark
Cover design by Bonnie Rose

Cover illustration: the author supervising the landing of a ZS2G-1 airship at Guantanamo Bay Cuba in 1957.

ISBN 9780692123348
LCCN 2018905862

Printed by Village Books in Bellingham, WA

to Anne

for fifty-three years of sunshine

SOME FAMILY BASICS

I grew up as a Mormon kid in Utah. Almost every kid I knew was a Mormon, except for my best friend and neighbor, Johnny Koroulis, whose Greek family did a separate Easter with maroon colored eggs and odd tasting cookies.

I was born in Salt Lake City in the spring of 1933. Lucky for me, in the midst of the Great Depression, my dad, Alton, had an office job at Utah Power and Light Company in Salt Lake City and my mom, Katherine, made us a good home on his modest income. We didn't seem to need much, living in Farmington. Mom said that was because we had "The Church." Partly, I guess. There's no arguing that growing up in that town of fifteen hundred fine folks, most of whom knew my name, gave me a real leg up. Times *were* bad but I had it good.

My 1933 world was decidedly low tech: We had no plastics, frozen foods, antibiotics, ballpoint pens, air conditioners, dishwashers, clothes dryers, FM radios, or televisions. We had adding machines and slide rules but couldn't imagine digital computers and their spawn (not until 1948 was the "bit" described and transistors invented). Still in the future were contact lenses, jet planes, helicopters, rap music (an oxymoron), and fast foods.

But for five cents each you could buy a bottle of Coke, an ice cream cone, a chocolate covered Milk Nickel, a Baby Ruth Candy Bar, or a box of Cracker Jacks that had a small prize hidden inside. Add a dime more and you could sit on a high stool at the drugstore soda fountain and sip through a straw a malted milkshake or a root beer float topped with whip cream and a cherry, presented in a tall, fluted, cone-shaped glass. But the best treat value by far was the big and delectable penny candy that you actually got to pick out yourself from one or more huge glass jars.

A nickel also bought an electric streetcar ride in Salt Lake City or a pay-phone call or an Air Mail stamp. Movies cost "two bits" (twenty-five cents) to four bits. Mom did a lot of her shopping in Salt Lake City's "five and dime" stores, like Kress and Woolworths. She considered anything made in Japan junk. Nothing was made in China, Bangladesh or Pakistan. A new Ford coupe cost about $500 but nobody in our town could afford one. If you did have a car, the gas was only 15 cents a gallon, but that seemed expensive to us. Keep in mind, my dad made less than $3,000 a year. Though some women worked as nurses, waitresses or secretaries—not called "executive assistants" then—few worked outside the home in any type of business and there were virtually no women in the professions. I was born on another planet, a world far away, just one step up from stone tools and saber tooth tigers.

My first name, Robert, was Mom's maiden name minus an "s". My middle name, Warren, first belonged to my paternal great grandfather, William Warren, a Civil War sergeant who, according to my brother Pat's book—*Sergeant Rose and the 115th Iowa in the War of the Rebellion*—helped General Sherman march through Georgia. When

I lived in Georgia, I never let on that Grandpa helped the General with that infamous assignment. Southern people are still really sensitive about that.

My paternal grandfather, William Warren Jr. —about whom I know very little—died when Dad was sixteen, so Dad quit high school to help support my grandma, Mabel, my uncle, Guy, and my aunt, Beth. Despite no college degree, or even a high school diploma, Dad became head of Business Development for Utah Power and Light Co. in Salt Lake City and was Mayor of Farmington for many years. He was writing his acceptance speech as the newly elected president of the Exchange Club, a prestigious Salt Lake City business executive's organization, when he suddenly died of a heart attack at age fifty-nine. His abrupt death devastated me and it was months before I stopped dreaming about him. Freud once wrote that the death of a man's father is the most important psychological event of his life—that a man only becomes a man on the day his father dies. Perhaps, but I could have put that off a while.

Unfortunately, Dad hadn't written anything about himself as Mom had. I guess he thought he had plenty of time.

Mom had to leave school after the eighth grade so she could work and help support her family. In spite of that, she was still able to attend the LDS Business College in Salt Lake City and was working at the Utah Power and Light Co. when she met very handsome and well-dressed Dad, a great dancer. Dad thought that Mom was pretty, had one hell of a figure, and was really smart. He was so smitten with her that he broke up with his then fiancé—a beauty who had helped him win many dancing contests, and whose father had helped him get his job—so that he could propose to Mom. My mom was an excellent mother, if a demanding one. She was determined that her kids would be civilized, well-educated, and successful, a tall order considering what she had to work with.

Mom died six years after Dad due to complications of Lupus and cardiac surgery. We were told that the operation was *necessary* because of worsening rheumatic fever-induced heart valve damage she'd sustained as a child. She died in the recovery room post-op. Though we all missed Mom, her chronic illness had given us more time to adjust to the inevitable.

My maternal grandmother, Maggie May, died when Mom was a very small girl so there was a stepmother in the mix. Annie was nice to me and I liked her, but my mom and her sisters (Sue, Betty, and Dora) gave Annie mixed reviews, averaging only two or three stars out of a possible ten. Mom's brother, Eugene, refused to vote because he thought he'd probably skew the results downward. Mom's dad, Hugh Roberts, was my only living grandpa. He also got mixed reviews from the sisters, partly because of his choice of their stepmother.

My one living great grandparent, Tom Pinder, was a small, quiet man with thinning silver hair, a shy smile, and a strong English accent. He always wore a tie and vest. Grandma Rose told me that he had been a famous cathedral organist and music director in Lincolnshire, England, before he had immigrated to Utah with his family. He was a sought-after organ teacher and had been invited to play the Mormon Tabernacle organ on several occasions. Grandma said that he might have become a tabernacle organist but his touch was ruined—whatever that means—playing piano in a dance band.

After me, my parents had four more boys at three-year intervals. Ronald died of heart disease in infancy. He was pale with a blue tint so I suspect that he had a congenital cyanotic heart disease, though no one ever said. Terry, Nick and Pat were born in order. The four of us who survived infancy graduated from Davis High School in Kaysville, Utah and then attended the University of Utah in Salt Lake City, all on scholarships: The Navy claimed me for a four-year, full ride NROTC program and each of my three brothers won four-year Utah Power and Light Co. scholarships in Electrical Engineering. Remarkable in that none of us seemed to be serious students early on.

Three of us graduated from the University of Utah: I in Architecture and Nick and Pat in Electrical Engineering. Unfortunately, Terry died in his junior year of college due complications of chronic glomerulonephritis, a kidney disease. In the final year of his life, he and I commuted to the University of Utah together in my old car, which had almost bald tires. As I was fixing—without much help from him—our second flat tire in one week, he told me that he was seriously considering getting a more reliable means of transportation. He was one smart and funny dude. Ironically, he died just a year or so before dialysis and kidney transplants became available.

Pat and I went on to get MD degrees and, after specialty training, went into medical practice in Pediatric Cardiology and Pediatrics respectively, though I soon flew the baby doctor nest to become a diagnostic radiologist. Nick got an MBA degree when it was unusual for an engineer to do so and ultimately became CEO of Questar Regulated Services, a four-state natural gas distribution company.

The folks would have been proud. Our parents considered higher education to be an absolute necessity for success in life and they worked for, prayed for, and *expected* us to be successful. After all, this was Mormon country and Mormons think like that.

LITTLE BOB

When I was about four years old, I locked my mom out of our rented house and couldn't figure out how to undo the damage, so Mom had to climb up and squeeze through an unlocked bathroom window to get back in. By then she was really mad, shouting that she had a bad heart—which it turned out she did—and that it was going to kill her—which it didn't for many years and only then because she had a little help from "Mack the Knife," her intrepid cardiac surgeon. But the fact that I almost killed my mom seriously plucked at my guilt strings—an easy pluck, as it's turned out.

There were no neighborhood kids, preschool hadn't been invented, and Junior Sunday School was only once a week, so my folks, thinking I was lonely, bought me a little white pup for a playmate. Whitey and I hit it right off and soon became inseparable pals as we ran, barked and giggled, around the house. I was over-the-moon happy and my parents were delighted.

But then Dad did the unthinkable: he snatched that pup from my lap, chopped off his tail, and dipped the stump in flour to stop the bleeding. My little white buddy was not a trooper. He yipped and yapped for quite some time and I blubbered right along with him. But as his wail subsided, I wiped my tears, puffed up my chest, wagged a finger at my dad, and shouted, "DON'T YOU *EVER* DO THAT AGAIN!"

SLIGHTLY BIGGER BOB

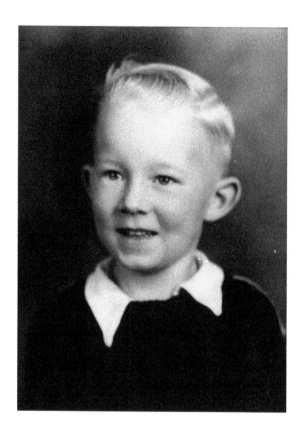

I had just turned five when we moved in with Grandma Rose, who lived across the "upper road" from the city cemetery in south Farmington. Large spring-blooming cherry, peach, and apricot orchards abutted the graveyard. These groves climbed the lower slopes of the scrub oak and sagebrush covered Wasatch mountain foothills to the east, the shores of old Lake Bonneville. Above these inclines, the mountains rose abruptly.

A vast Concord grape vineyard adjoined the south side of my grandmother's property. Because of the fruit's lip-smacking flavor and abundance, I had better grape jelly and peanut butter sandwiches than any of my friends.

Sloping down gently to the west were pastures and cornfields hiding coveys of quail and bouquets of pheasants. Small spring-fed streams filled with watercress, spring tadpoles, and darting minnows, burbled through these fields. In the far west, model-like cars and trucks motored on the "lower road" and steam engines pulled strings of cars between Salt Lake City and Ogden on the Union Pacific railroad tracks. The Great Salt Lake and Antelope Island fused with the sunset.

We were *almost* surrounded by beauty. But sadly, abutting our property to the north was the Neuman's commercial chicken ranch: two large ominous, dirty-white, low-gabled buildings with a few window slits punched high in the walls. The relative lack of windows was fortunate because the interior lights stayed on twenty-four/seven in that chicken and egg producing free-range operation of our day. Leafy trees, bushes, and weeds partially masked the dark process from our house until fall when denuded limbs and stems exposed large brown mounds of chicken excrement. Mercifully, we seldom caught the smell of those piles because the wind rarely blew from true north.

One memorable morning, the chicken coop fronting the road was swept out and Mr. Newman, who'd been a baker before emigrating from Germany, opened The Breadbasket. The bakery became quite popular as "a nice drive for great bread" for Salt Lake City folks, who lived thirty miles to the south. Made us wonder if we locals got the same bread they did because Mrs. Neuman's "fresh" bread concept could be a crap-shoot. But Mr. Neuman made killer alligators and bear claws and his marzipan was the best ever. When the bakery replaced the chicken coop our land value soared.

Fascinating but repulsive was the Neuman's three-hole outdoor toilet behind their nearby house. I always worried that a black widow spider would find my soft parts inviting, so, though I often played with the Neuman kids, I used their restroom facility (and the Montgomery Ward catalog that they used for toilet paper) sparingly. An adjacent, poorly covered old cesspool was equally uninviting. Because I occasionally had nightmares about falling into that big smelly cesspit—a *disgusting* way to go—I gave it a wide berth.

Mr. Neuman had an old Model T Ford that was usually in disrepair, but on one occasion he got it all together and offered Mom and me a ride to Salt Lake City. I had to sit on the back seat where I was lined up behind a large gap in the floorboards. Mom's major complaint was that he drove the whole trip at 25 miles an hour, but I kept thinking about what it would be like to fall through that gaping hole onto the concrete road whizzing by beneath us.

The economy was still severely depressed in those late 1930s. Even though my Dad had a job, we had to economize, as did most families we knew. Mom mended our clothes as necessary. I was a pretty active kid, so most of my overalls and jeans had knee patches, but I didn't care because my friends' pants were patched too. My mom also darned the holes in my socks and told me to not take off my shoes in public. She darned Dad's socks too but I don't know what she told him.

A few of my friends lived in basement houses covered with flat tar-paper roofs because their families couldn't afford to build above the foundation. When I learned that we were going to build a house, I assumed we'd be living in a basement too for a while. But Dad assured me that our house would have walls, windows, and a gabled roof, like most people's homes around town did. I was somewhat relieved that we'd be living above ground.

We moved in with Grandma Rose while Dad and Mom were planning our new home, which would be built between my grandmother's house and the chicken coop/bakery. Grandma's crank-up wall phone number was "41J," a party line. It was weird to pick up the phone and hear other people talking about their lives. "Get off the phone, Bob" was a phrase I heard pretty often. We knew all of the telephone operators by name, and where they lived. Because of their vocation, they knew pretty much everything about us. The switchboard girls were about as excited about our new home plans as we were, and one of them would check in with us periodically, just to see how things were coming along.

To finance our house, Dad got a three-percent home loan from Mr. Palmer. I would often accompany my dad when he went to Mr. Palmer's house with a payment, but I always had to wait in the car. Mr. Palmer stood back in the shadows, so I never got a good look at the man. I imagined he was something like Ebenezer Scrooge, the only other money man I knew about. Why Dad didn't just drop a check in the mail I don't know, but perhaps Mr. Palmer preferred cash for tax purposes.

On the day construction began, I sat cross-legged on a big mound of dirt and watched Dad and Uncle Guy manhandle a large steel scoop—towed by two large plodding, sweaty workhorses—as they dug out the basement of our soon-to-be house.

Larry Benoit, a carpenter friend of Dad's, then built us a beautiful white stucco two-bedroom home with a gabled roof (as promised), red brick chimneys, and an unfinished basement. At $3000, it had to be the deal of a lifetime. I especially liked the large boxy concrete front porch, from which my cousins and I would hurl ourselves out into space to test our homemade Superman capes. In the summer, we'd sit with our legs hanging over the porch-edge while we watched the moon rise over the mountains above the cemetery, counted fireflies, and swatted the occasional mosquito.

A lump-coal-burning furnace in the basement heated our home initially. It was connected to registers in the rooms by large metal convection ducts. Coal had to be shoveled into the furnace throughout each day and clinker residue removed, both messy jobs. Eventually, a worm gear stoker was added, which slowly fed pea-coal (small crushed coal pieces) into the furnace from a hopper that only had to be filled once a day. That addition made clinker duty a joy. Finally, the coal heat system was replaced with natural gas, which not only eliminated the clinkers, but also allowed Dad to build a special bedroom—for the oldest student living at home—in the large basement space that had previously held coal. My three brothers and I all used that bedroom in turn.

Dad remodeled the basement as family needs dictated, doing most of the work himself. In addition to the student bedroom, he built a family room, which he much later divided into two bedrooms, and a large pantry for storing the many bottles of fruits and vegetables my folks "put-up" (bottled) each summer. But my father's supreme labor of love was a beautiful one car stone garage that he eventually built on the chicken ranch side of the house. He used multicolored native stone, mostly granite, that he had hand-selected and gathered from Farmington's several mountain creek flood zones.

The next best thing to living with my grandmother was living next door to her. Grandma, her hair in a tight bun, always started my day off right: She'd peer over her rimless glasses, worn low on her nose, and say, "What do you want for breakfast, Bob?" Then, in a pan of sizzling bacon grease on the top of an old wood-burning stove, she'd cook me bacon, sunny side-up eggs, and cut-up potatoes. She'd serve that delicious combination with buttered toast, homemade jam, and a big glass of milk poured from a long-necked bottle that had to be shaken because the cream had floated to the top. We didn't know about fat and cholesterol then.

Grandma's Sunday dinners were to die for (perhaps a poor choice of words): roast beef, Yorkshire pudding, mashed potatoes with thick gravy, one or two fresh or put-up vegetables from our garden, Parker House rolls, and cake or pie for desert. She taught her daughter, sons, and all of their spouses to prepare this meal, with minor variations. It could be started before church and quickly finished after the services. Because Mormon meetings were long, and there was fasting till noon once a month, the Sunday dinner was always something for me to look forward to while my mind was wandering, praying for church to end.

Sometimes I was put to bed in Grandma's east bedroom, which had a large picture window facing the cemetery and nearby mountains. Trying to sleep, I could often hear the bark and yip-yapping wail of coyotes, or the rare howl of a wolf. Unfortunately, on the wall of this same bedroom was a menacing blue-gray picture of a howling wolf on a hill that everyone's grandma had on a wall—not too reassuring when there's only one thin pane of glass between you and what's out there.

Grandma's screened-in sleeping porch was great in the summer. I could contemplate the stars, the moon, darting bats, and flitting fireflies. A corrugated tin roof amplified the comforting sound of pattering rain, hastening sleep on a good night. But thunderstorms were another matter; blinding lightning flashes danced around the room and the crash of thunder rattled those old galvanized steel roof plates like orchestra cymbals. I would vamoose, pronto!

My grandma and I watched the only live tornado I've ever seen as it touched down in Centerville, four or five miles south of us. The twister, a rare occurrence for the Wasatch Front, picked up the roof of Centerville's elementary school and set it down in a nearby pasture, injuring no one. It was also rumored to have swept up a few cows and returned them to earth unharmed…yeah, sure.

Grandma and I would sometimes get all duded up and take the "Bamberger Electric" commuter trolley train to Salt Lake City to do some shopping. We usually stopped at the Kress or Woolworths five and dimes. These were my favorite stores because they had cheap little toys that I could sometimes con Grandma into buying. As we inhaled the lunch counter's mouth-watering smells, we'd sit on high padded stools at Woolworths and invariably order hot turkey sandwiches that came with mashed potatoes, thick brown gravy, and mixed vegetables. Yum. We'd briefly visit my dad at his desk in the Utah Power and Light building and then go to a movie. We saw the maiden runs of *Snow White and the Seven Dwarfs,* the first full-length animated movie ever, and *Bambi,* which made deer seem just like folks. That movie became my deer hunting nemesis.

If I was lucky, Grandma might top off the Salt Lake trip with a visit to the shoe store, so I could peer into their new shoe-fitting fluoroscope and watch my toe bones move. That was certainly unhealthy for me, or anyone else looking through the view ports of that poorly shielded x-ray device, but it sure was fascinating and helped folks get a better shoe fit, we were told.

In contrast to those outings with Grandma, trips to town with Mom were hurry-up things, shopping for school clothes, and the like. They certainly did not include kid movies or toy purchases. I did like it when she'd take me to Auerbachs's, for "real quality," because they had extremely beautiful, uniformed female elevator operators that smelled good too.

On any trip to Salt Lake City with Grandma, or Mom, I'd pray we'd run into "Pa," a charming dapper elderly man who wore pince-nez glasses low on his nose. Though a distant relative, he always made a fuss over me in his kid-oriented Dutch accent (if you can imagine such a thing). After making a show about not remembering which pocket it was in, he would invariably produce a shiny new silver dollar that he'd hold out to me between two fingers, like a magician. I'd almost swoon. Miraculously, we seemed to run into Pa almost every time we came to downtown Salt Lake City, which I never thought strange until I was writing this vignette. Do you think Grandma and Mom were in cahoots with him and let him know when we were coming to town? Perhaps, but no one ever said a word about it.

Mom had a favorite Grandma story: soon after we had moved into our new home, my mother grabbed a little switch and started chasing me for some transgression du jour. She usually caught me but on this particular day my feet had wings. I left Mom in the dust as I scampered around the far side of Grandma's house, through her open kitchen door, past Grandma working at the stove ("Help, Grandma!"), and into Grandma's bedroom where I scooted under the bed. Mom came to the door and said, "Mabel, have you seen Bob?" With a straight face, my grandmother replied, "No, Katherine, I haven't seen him all day." Later, Mom told Aunt Barbara, "I couldn't believe that she'd lie for that little stinker but what could I do?"

Family vacations were not frequent, so a few were memorable: on a family vacation to California in the late 1930s, our car's radiator boiled over in the middle of the forbidding Mohave Desert. We spent the better part of a very hot morning filling the old automobile's steaming radiator with water, mercifully donated by passing motorists, and inching our way, between engine vapor locks, to an ever-distant gas station. Fortunately, most service stations in those days carried fan belts for the few car makes that were on the road, so we were eventually on our way again. But seeing my folks truly worried left me feeling that fan belts were super-serious stuff, so I always asked Dad if he had a spare one before we left home on any road trip.

Our rare highway adventures beyond the Wasatch Front were usually to Idaho, where Grandpa Hugh had his farm. As soon as we crossed the Utah/Idaho border, I'd start lobbying for a side trip picnic at Soda Springs. Don't get me wrong, I enjoyed riding plow horses, swimming in the canal, and throwing cow pies at my cousins. But how often can you see the largest captive carbon dioxide generated cold-water geyser in the world, one that erupts with an impressive jet of carbonated water "every hour on the hour"? With a little Kool Aid, sugar, and maybe some lemon, I could make everyone their favorite flavored soda pop for lunch, using that wondrous sparkling water that we'd just seen magically erupting up out of the earth…a kid's dream.

Grandpa Hugh, and other farmers in Southern Idaho, considered jackrabbits a scourge, particularly in the summer when rabbit numbers multiplied to the point that they would devastate several acres of crops in a single night. Even bunny-lover Dad had no problem shooting as many of these large-eared pests as possible, a task made easier at night when suddenly switched-on car headlights would illuminate a virtual sea of momentarily immobilized rabbits—a thousand eyes a-shining.

Desperate farmers resorted to rabbit drives because they couldn't make a dent in the rabbit population with firearms. I got to tag along behind Dad and Mom's half-brother, David, on one of these gruesome events. I was even issued a stick so I could join a wide ring of grim-faced, club-wielding farmers as they bludgeoned hundreds of jackrabbits and drove many hundreds more toward a wire enclosure where they could be contained and clubbed to death. Kids were expected to issue the coup de grace on those rabbits only stunned. It was easy to get in the spirit of things and I soon found myself clubbing at those bunnies with the best of them—not pleasant, but necessary...right? As our grim-faced, all-volunteer army left the killing field, I looked back to see men filling trucks with rabbit carcasses. Someone nearby said, "I'll bet your kid will remember this for the rest of his life, Alton."

Another great Idaho trip was to Aunt Barbara's dad's cattle ranch near Bancroft, Idaho, where I got to play cowboy for a few days. I considered ranching cooler than dirt farming because in the movies we saw that the Indians were always killing the male farmers and stealing their women. This forced the ranchers to round up a posse and go after the farmers' womenfolk, at least the younger ones.

After my breakfast steak one morning (another reason I liked ranching), I got to ride a horse behind old Bud Stoddard as he took me, and some other hands, out to see some cows branded and a quarter horse broken. But the thing I most remember about that trip was a visit to a pig farm where the pigs lived on concrete floors that were hosed down each day. We were told that pigs were basically clean animals that gained weight faster out of the feces-laden mud, as long as they had shade to keep the sun off their sensitive skin. Our pigs at home didn't know what they were missing, but they got to live longer.

Now a bit about doctoring: I was told that I almost died of whooping cough. A few kids did. But surviving that must not have been good enough, because when I was five years old, Doc Buchanan decided that my future good health required a tonsillectomy. Rather than doing it in a facility with an anesthesiologist (rarely done in those days), he cut them out in his office while Dad slowly dripped chloroform onto a facemask to keep me asleep. I learned later that chloroform is a dangerous old anesthetic, not used anymore, that can produce vomiting, aspiration, liver damage, convulsions, and respiratory and cardiac arrest. Oh...and I could have bled to death. The stars must have been in proper alignment that day.

But to Doc Buchanan's credit, near the end of the Second World War he gave me some of the first penicillin available for civilian use. "It saved your life," said Mom, referring to my pneumonia's dramatic response to that new wonder drug. Penicillin was first made from bread mold fungus, but was probably mass-produced in cantaloupe or corn steep liquor by the time I got it. All I remember about the miracle was that I had two or three days of severe buttock pain due to the injection of that early beeswax-containing substance into my very small rear end.

The tonsil issue was revisited during my last year of college: Farmington's then general practitioner, Doc Jenson, suggested that I should have some remaining tonsil tags removed. You can see that tonsil tissue was considered a sinister threat in my hometown…like the vapors were in the 19th century. "No need to make a big deal out of it," he said as he sat me in a chair, handed me a pan to hold the excised fragments, injected Novocain around my throat, and started snipping away. I remember thinking how amazing it was that he could cut out all those small pieces of flesh and I couldn't feel a thing…and then the Novocain wore off!

For most illnesses, Mom was the family doctor. She believed that for colds and coughs I needed to have pungent, foul-smelling Vicks VapoRub applied to my chest, or inhale Vick's fumes from a water bath, or wear a Vicks alcohol pack around my neck… the smell still haunts me. If my cough needed "loosening-up," I might get a mustard plaster or two applied to my chest. That ageless homemade poultice was hot, miserably uncomfortable, and, as we now know, medically useless. Mom can be forgiven for using it in the 1930s and 1940s, particularly if Aunt Betty, the family shaman, suggested it. But I still see it touted on quackery sites today. Like bloodletting, it never completely goes away.

As a little kid, I had seen no live non-church entertainment, so when Dad and Uncle Guy took five-year-old me to the Ringling Brothers and Barnham and Bailey Circus ("The Greatest Show on Earth"), performed outdoors in a gigantic three-ring tent, with *live* animals, I was beside myself with joy. As we were leaving the tent, Uncle Guy bought me a multicolored feathered bird on a string that made a whistling sound as you twirled it around your head. I thought I would faint away.

Not a three-ring-circus, but certainly memorable, was a Junior Sunday School Easter program performed on the big elevated curtained stage of our church recreation room. I was a crepe paper hollyhock standing on a chair in the back row with other male flowers as we sang "In Grandmother's Old-Fashioned Garden." As Grandmother, a peer of ours, began watering the vegetation, tall and short, with her large fake watering can, tittering could be heard from the flowers on the chairs. Some sharp-eyed fellow hollyhock had spotted a widening puddle of real water forming around the feet of an extremely nervous petunia in the front row. Mom was not amused by our amusement.

Mom loved Fred Astaire, so she decided that I should learn to tap dance and be part of our church's entertainment pool. I took group lessons in the basement of the Davis County courthouse with a bunch of other kids my age. I soon found that I was more interested in the World War One guns and uniforms in the courthouse display cases than I was in the tap dancing, but I still gave it a jolly good effort. I could eventually do a crude "Shuffle Off to Buffalo" and the like. Dad attended my first performance and immediately noticed that I was the *only* boy, was dressed in red and white satin, was wearing black patent leather dance shoes, and had been slathered with lipstick and rouge. That was pretty much it for dancing.

Dad had strong feelings about our masculinity training. I reported to my parents that I had seen one of my male cousins sit down and face the back of the toilet as he urinated—"So that I won't splash," he'd explained to me. My mother thought that the act showed consideration for his mother, but Dad thought otherwise: "If I ever catch one of my boys doing that he'll have to go outside for a week, rain or shine.

YOUTHFUL BOB

There was a lot of kid freedom in our small, rural, predominantly Mormon town. As far as we knew, child molestation and abduction were not serious threats, so we rarely had adult supervision. When I became scout age, I was pretty much allowed to roam the fields and foothills at will.

But the church took up an awfully big chunk of my non-school time. There were Sunday school meetings, priesthood meetings, Sunday night sacrament meetings, monthly fast meetings, and weekly MIA (Mutual Improvement Association) meetings. Fortunately, my scout troop was considered mutual improvement, which allowed me a little non-scripture-based fun.

If I behaved myself during those long Sunday meetings, I could sit with friends and try to pass the time faster by adding phrases such as "between the sheets" to the end of hymnal song titles like "Come, Come Ye Saints" or "We Are All Enlisted." We'd also play Hangman or Tick Tack Toe, anything that could be done quietly. That definitely meant *no* snickering and laughing, or we'd have to sit with our folks.

But all of us boys would come alive during Sunday school's hymn request time, because we could choose "Put Your Shoulder to The Wheel," or some similar foot-stomper, and get the blood moving. The adult hymnal choices were a definite step up from "Jesus Wants Me for a Sunbeam," one of the few selections offered in Junior Sunday School.

We Saints must have all been immersed in the spirit one wintry Sunday morning because thieves entered our church's large cloakroom and made off with all the coats without anyone noticing. They tossed the cloaks out of the restroom window, loaded them into a truck in the parking lot, and drove away. Can you believe that no one saw that dastardly deed being committed and the crooks got away? A witness wouldn't have been much help in Farmington, because we only had one part-time policeman, and he was only predictably available in the summer, when the Lagoon resort was open.

Speaking of immersion, the Mormons believe in that method of Baptism. I really liked being baptized for the dead (something Mormons do) in the Salt Lake City Temple. After a short prayer, they'd dunk me in a large baptismal font that sat atop twelve huge golden oxen. I really thought I could hear those dead people thanking me.

I loved Temple Square. Looking at the old Indian mummy in the glass case at the Pioneer Museum never grew old. As part of a church-wide youth chorus performance, I once sat in one of the Tabernacle Choir's seats and helped belt out "How Firm a Foundation," accompanied by the Alexander Schreiner on the Tabernacle organ, a once-in-a-lifetime experience. But it could be embarrassing to be in the congregation at Priesthood Conference in the Tabernacle, singing along-side my Grandpa Hugh; he always sang out each hymn at full volume, sometimes off key, and often through a pause in the music—when the other twelve thousand voices in that sound-enhancing chamber were silent! But he was my grandpa and I loved him.

Mormons have no paid clergy, so guess who helps fill that gap? Kids were often assigned the "Two and One Half Minute Talk" to ostensibly make them better public speakers. I usually went to the restroom when they were looking for volunteers, but they occasionally tagged me anyway.

Edgar A. Guest authored a poem I recited at one of these events. It's interesting that I can remember old Edgar's name now, because I surely forgot it that day: "Ahh...written by..., Ahh...written by..., Ahh...well anyway...." Then the mental clouds cleared. I got it together and delivered the poem flawlessly. Most parents would have been happy with that, but not *my* mom. From the car's passenger seat, looking straight ahead, she said, "Bob, maybe you could have prepared better." I thought: *Edgar A. Guest, Edgar A. Poe, who cares?* But the guilt card had been played—trump around our house—so I gave it a few extra licks next time and even brought notes, a first for me.

There were no movie theaters in Farmington, so the church ward house was the center for celluloid entertainment. Biweekly, Dwain Bybee would set up two old theater-type carbon arc lamp movie projectors in the recreation room projection booth, pull down a huge end-wall movie screen, and set up folding chairs on the basketball court's protective canvas because—it was "Movie Night"!

We saw a lot of cowboy movies, usually starring Gene Autry or Roy Rogers, but Dwain sometimes surprised us with a good second-run film. He always made sure that we had accompanying cartoons or comedy shorts, often starring The Three Stooges, The Marx Brothers, or Laurel and Hardy. During WWII, we often had newsreels, but the war had usually progressed far beyond Dwain's old news flicks.

The custom in the fifth and sixth grades was to walk a girl to and from the movies. Once the lights were dimmed and the movie was playing, a guy would put his arm on the back of his girl's folding chair, all the while looking straight ahead, ostensibly watching the movie. That accomplished, he'd try to lean over and plant a kiss on his date's cheek. If he succeeded, he got to tear one tooth per kiss out of his comb, which he would show to the rest of us the next day. Unfortunately, we had to give up the practice because we found the honor system didn't work. There was no way that some of those guys could have sneaked in all those kisses the rest of us hadn't seen.

On rare occasions, Dad would bring home one of Utah Power and Light Company's 16mm movie projectors, and a movie screen, and invite a few friends over to see some of the electric utility's full-color public-service movies. This was in the days before TV and affordable movie cameras, so a show-at-home flick of any kind was a big deal. We all loved *Clean Water*, a movie that dramatically explained how the power company was thinking about us when they built their hydroelectric dams and helped us treat our water supplies. Man, we were glued to the screen and asked Dad to play that hour-long documentary film twice. In spite of the smorgasbord of TV shows and DVDs my grandkids have available to them now, I'd bet they'd like *Clean Water* as much as we did.

The yearly ward dinners were great. The Women's Relief Society cooked these feasts in the church's recreation room kitchen. To a kid, these were about as scrumptious as you could get: roast beef, mashed potatoes, fresh Parker House rolls, canned green beans or corn, Jell-O fruit salad, and cake or pie for desert. After dinner, we folded up and put away the chairs and long tables and rolled up the basketball court's canvas covering so that dancing to a live six-man band could begin. That's where Mom and Dad really shined. They were far and away the best dancers in town. I can never remember anyone but Dad being the master-of-ceremonies at these soirees, or for that matter, at any other church recreation event. Dad had jokes for any occasion, and could always make you laugh, even if you had heard it all before.

For events like the dinners, and for most church meetings, a young man had to have a suit. So, Dad and I would go to Heusted and Montague, my dad's tailors, where they'd take my measurements and make me one. Dad said they gave him a good price because I was so skinny. A suit required a tie and a four-point folded breast pocket-handkerchief, so Dad taught me how to fold the hanky and make a Windsor tie knot, a harder chore than the fore-and-hand knot the Navy later required (the modern Navy has shifted to Windsor knots for Dress Blue uniforms). Recently, I was complimented for my Windsor knot and asked where I'd learned to tie it. I replied that my father had taught me and I had taught my two boys, adding, "It's just a thing dads do in the Rose family."

Dad took pride in his appearance. Each day he carefully spotted and ironed his suit and a fresh pocket-handkerchief, using a damp cloth for steam. Mom washed and ironed our shirts and pants (no permanent press then), our sheets and pillowcases, our underwear, and anything else she thought needed ironing. Most moms we knew did. Dad was always worrying about Mom's rheumatic heart condition, so he eventually bought her a sit-down drum ironer. He was very proud of it and would often sit and do a load of laundry himself. "He must love you Katherine," said Aunt Sue, paying Dad one of her rare compliments—and indeed he did.

I was an enthusiastic reader of chapter books, like Albert Payson Terhune's *Lad: A Dog* and *Buff: A Collie*, but what we called "funny books" (ten cent comic books) were my passion. I had boxes of comics stored under my bed that I could whip out to show my friends at a moment's notice. This was superhero birth-time, so I couldn't wait to get to Rampton drugstore to buy new issues of *Superman, Dick Tracy, Batman, Captain Marvel, Captain Midnight, Buck Rogers,* and *Wonder Woman.* With the arrival of *Captain America, Spiderman,* and *The Hulk,* Mr. Rampton had to put up a new shelf. He soon added a third shelf for less-super, but still good, *Li'l Abner, Looney Tunes, Mickey Mouse, Blondie, Little Orphan Annie and Prince Valiant.* I was only able to kick my habit of looking under the bed at bedtime (not sure what I expected to see...or what I'd do if I saw anything) when my many boxes of comic books filled most of the under-bed space.

I was the very proud owner of a first edition of Action Comics (1938) that introduced Superman to the world. Johnny Koroulis and I loved that one, and we'd reread it every so often. A single copy of that comic book recently sold for over three million dollars, so I'll bet Mom is sorry she gave away all of my comics when I went in the Navy. I hope to ask her about that someday.

We had no TV but we had radio, so we'd make up the picture in our heads. I'd run home from school so I could listen to my radio programs: *Buck Rogers, Sky King, Superman, Captain Midnight,* and *Jack Armstrong, the All-American Boy.*

Unfortunately, a few of these were on different radio stations at the same time, so choices had to be made…but only after I'd carefully considered what mail-in box top premiums competing programs were offering. I always kept a supply of Wheaties box tops and Ovaltine inner seals on hand, because Jack Armstrong and Captain Midnight seemed to offer the best and most frequent prizes. One of the all-time best premiums offered was the Sky King Secret Signalscope, which boasted a glow in the dark signaling device, a whistle, a magnifying glass, a private code, and the ability to see around corners and trees. All of this could be had for fifteen cents and the inner seal of a jar of Peter Pan Peanut Butter. Like Ralphy in *A Christmas Story*, I found that these longed-for treasures were usually better to dream about than actually get.

On evenings or weekends, radio dramas such as *I Love a Mystery, The Shadow, Gangbusters, Grand Central Station,* and *The FBI in Peace and War* might attract adults to listen to the radio with me, as would comedy shows such as *Jack Benny, Bob Hope, Fibber McGee and Molly,* and *Edgar Bergan and Charley McCarthy*. Why a ventriloquist and his dummy (on the radio of all things) would have appealed to us listeners is beyond me. But McGee's closet crashing down as he opened its door is still a classic. I think of McGee and laugh every time that happens to me.

My parents bought a TV set while I was in the Navy and that was it for the radio. Dad loved that little black and white TV tube. It became the new family gathering place.

For three long years, I sporadically took classical piano lessons, part of Mom's continuing effort to make me a cultured gentleman. My reward for suffering through those *John W. Schaum Piano Course* lesson books was an invitation to spend a long weekend at my piano teacher's farm in North Davis County. I think that my mentor felt guilty for suggesting that our time (and Mom's money) could be better spent. I wouldn't be surprised to learn that my desperate keyboard coach had been contemplating having me give a poem rather than tickle the ivories at the next piano recital.

I enjoyed the mini-vacation at my teacher's farm until her boys enthusiastically suggested that I learn to ride a horse…bareback no less. "Our most gentle horse" turned into a rodeo bronc with me on its naked back. Trotting without stirrups crushed my private parts and the horse threw me twice before I painfully refused to get back on. Understand, I *love* horses, but only if someone else is riding them. *Warhorse* was a fantastic movie and *Seabiscuit* is one of my all-time favorites. I still maintain that there's never been a *bad* cowboy movie, though this premise was repeatedly challenged by some of Dwain Bybee's church recreation room flicks.

To her credit, Mom never gave up on the piano thing. While I was in high school, she somehow discovered Wally Williams, a mostly retired big band pianist, who taught piano chord structure and embellishments. Now this was more like it. Unfortunately, my many high school activities precluded my giving Wally's keyboard method the attention it deserved at the time, but I got considerable mileage with it later on, and a lot of Wally intangibles that were priceless. Wally always had a new joke or two, which he told with great gusto at the end of each early evening session. After our joke swap, he would whip out a telescope on a tripod, turn out the lights, and we would scan the windows of the lower five floors of the Hotel Utah, which was directly across the street from his Salt Lake City studio. Believe me, Katherine got more for her education dollars than she could ever imagine.

But a bit more about Dad: He was a brilliant and likeable guy, a natural leader, whom everyone wanted on their committee or board. While mayor of Farmington, he was elected president of the Utah Municipal League (now the Utah League of Cities and Towns). He helped found Farmington's Lions Club and served as its president for several years. One of his many business honors was the previously mentioned Salt Lake City Exchange Club presidency to which he had just been elected before he died. Church officials kept meeting with Dad, hoping to coax him to higher office.

Dad was also a hands-on guy. Farmington couldn't afford a full-time maintenance man while my dad was mayor, so to save the city money—at least that's what he said—he decided to drive the city's newly purchased second-hand diesel road grader from Salt Lake City to Farmington, using as many dirt roads as he could find. He took me along on that dusty six-hour trip and even let me drive that behemoth while sitting on his lap. We pulled into a cow pasture to eat our sack lunches, but didn't get off the grader because there was a huge bull across the field menacingly watching us. Cow farmers used bulls then, not just sperm syringes.

Radio broadcasts of the Salt Lake City Bees baseball games were a favorite of Dad's and mine, particularly on warm summer nights when we could work or sit outside. Away games were "recreated" by an excited KSL announcer who made up the action of each game—dubbing in crowd noise and the bat connecting with the ball—as he watched a ticker tape account of the ongoing event in a far-away city such as Denver. The guy was so good at his craft it was hard to tell the recreated games from the real ones played in Salt Lake City. Once or twice a summer, we'd go to a real game, which helped us visualize the radio drama.

We only fished with worms and spinners before I went in the Navy. Dad later learned to fly fish and taught the art to my brothers, lucky guys. There's something romantic about being able to snap and dance a hairy fly you've created onto some fish's watery dinner table, but bait fishing probably better suited my personality. I loved to sit on big boulders, or wade in rippling mountain streams, as I tried to work that drowned bait around rocks and snags and into each swirling fishing hole where those dark, darting creatures were likely to be feeding. At lunchtime, I would find a rock to lean against while I gazed at the shimmering tree canopy, listened to a gurgling stream, or a crashing waterfall, and ate the fine-tasting lunch I'd been carrying in my creel all morning. The mirrored still water of a high mountain lake was a dreamlike world until there was a fish on—then it was a battlefield! (One of my favorite entertaining books on the subject is *The River Why*[1] by David James Duncan.)

I was a pretty good shot with Dad's open iron sight (we couldn't afford scopes in those days) 32 special lever-action rifle, so, when I turned sixteen, I was welcomed into the yearly family deer hunting encampment in the mountains high above Farmington. I liked to camp with the gang, and I loved deer meat, so I contributed to the combined larders for two straight years before I got the Bambi Syndrome—those big brown eyes just made deer seem like folks to me. Uncle Howard didn't agree and didn't appreciate my missing the easy shots, particularly the big four-point buck he'd driven my way: "Do you think the kid needs glasses, Alton?"

I should have seen that weakness creeping up on me. The malady had made me give up shooting at squirrels and chipmunks with my cool Winchester pump 22-rifle I'd bought with my fruit picking money. I mostly settled for "plinking" cans and bottles, probably even more fun, truth be told. But I reserved the right to shoot at magpies. There were no movies suggesting that those screeching, black and white, crow-like pests were loveable, so I considered them fair game. I'd heard that a magpie could be trained to talk, so I really hoped I could mildly wound one and capture it. But those mocking magpies weren't worried. The crafty creatures seemed to know the second I squeezed the trigger, and would swoop off, middle claw extended. Then they'd land close by and taunt me.

The Grabeteria was a stand-up, only, businessmen's lunch shop in downtown Salt Lake City that had each day's newspapers tacked up on its walls and partitions above the elongated waist-high lunch shelves. A couple of a times a year, I would take the Bamberger train or bus to Salt Lake City, pick up Dad at the Utah Power and Light Co., and we'd eat our lunch at the Grabeteria…anything I wanted! Then it was over to nearby Temple Square to listen to the noontime organ recital in the Mormon Tabernacle. Our favorite organist was Alexander Schreiner because he seldom played

---

[1] Duncan, David James, *The River Why*, Sierra Clubs Books, 1983.

Bach. The Tabernacle's other organist, Frank Asper, played Bach's compositions relentlessly.

Though I had those fine lunches with Dad, and delicious meals at Woolworths with Mom or Grandma, I can't remember our whole family going to a sit-down restaurant before I went into the Navy. This was in part due to family economics, but also, there just weren't any restaurants close by. Fast food joints ("restaurants" by loose definition) had not been invented yet. Can you imagine a world without the golden arches? Of course, "drive-ins" were present in the larger Davis County towns. You got to stay in your car for these, and we *loved* our cars. At the driver's side window, cute high school girls would place trays on the side of our automobile before they took and delivered our order. When things were slow, they might even lean in to chat and joke it up a bit, because we mostly knew each other. Sadly, drive-ins have almost disappeared with the advent of the fast food eateries and their take-out windows.

Dad loved Christmas. So regardless of the weather, the weekend after Thanksgiving he was always downtown helping Barney Thomas put up the city's Christmas lights. Above Main Street were crisscrossing strings of multicolored lightbulbs that connected to white light strings and a star above our town's major intersection. An illuminated crèche beneath a huge decorated spruce tree on the Courthouse lawn, and lighted Christmas scenes on the streetlight poles, helped Farmington's Yuletide light display become a state small town award winner. There was nothing finer than our downtown at night during the Christmas season, particularly when it was snowing. Farmingtonians felt that it was right up there with Salt Lake City's lavish display, which most Mormons, at least, thought was really something.

The Salvation Army in Idaho had provided very-young Mom her *only* Christmas present one year when my grandpa was forced to move his family, and their tent, from farm to farm to find work. Because of this, making Christmas special for us kids was as important to Mom as it was to Dad. They made it so much fun that I didn't let on that I knew about Santa until my eleventh Christmas, when that jolly old elf gave me a Lionel train set on a large train table that Dad had built, painted, and decorated in the basement, all the while trying to keep it hidden from me. Exhausted by the effort, he finally said, "You know Son, there's something your mother and I think that we ought to tell you...."

Each day between Thanksgiving and Christmas, Salt Lake City's *The Deseret News* would print a small seasonal scene on its cartoon page, reminding us readers—in very large font—how many shopping days remained until Christmas—essentially a serialized commercial version of an advent calendar. I couldn't wait for the paperboy to get there each afternoon, even though I knew what the number would be.

As the big day got closer, I would lie under our Christmas tree looking up at the lights, the multicolored mirrored balls, and other special ornaments, and the excitement would build. By Christmas Eve, I was higher than a kite. I'd get down on my knees and pray for sleep—forget it. I'd count sheep, sometimes up to a thousand—no help. Around four or five o-clock in the morning I'd finally crash, only to be awakened two hours later by my mom and dad who liked to start Christmas before dawn. My folks thought that the tree lights and the glowing windows of the Christmas village on the fireplace mantel would make the first sight of toys and presents truly magical...and it always did.

My favorite present from Santa was a large Erector set with a *real* electric motor, a definite step up from Lincoln Logs. At last, I could build things that really did something.

Personal radios were hard to come by and were expensive, so, using a kit I got as a Christmas present, I built a cheap crystal set with earphones. By positioning the needle at just the right place on the pyrite crystal, and moving the ground wire between painted and unpainted surfaces on a galvanized steel water pipe, I was able to get two radio stations. This irked my friends who also had crystal sets but could only get one station no matter what they did. Don't ask me why it worked—probably just some ionospheric curiosity.

One Christmas, Johnny Koroulis and I almost "bought the farm" with one of Santa's presents. We tried to make a bomb by mixing together the contents of several of those little wooden containers we found in my big wooden chemistry set case. Admittedly, the box had "adult supervision recommended" in big letters on the label. Fortunately, because of guys like us they made those sets pretty anemic, so, though some of our mixtures boiled over, and the bomb concoction even caught fire, none exploded in our unprotected faces.

My friend, Dean Kynaston, and his father enjoyed cars and working on cars. Dean's family was the first in town to buy a new auto after WWII, a maroon Mercury four-door sedan. Dean's dad would let us sit in the vehicle at night and turn on the fancy lighted dashboard radio. We'd listen to big band music and drink in the new-car smell, the first time any of us had been exposed to it. Though we were all too young to drive, we took turns at the wheel, telling each other where we were going, which girls we had with us, and what to expect. Then we'd laugh ourselves silly and switch drivers.

Dean was a few months older, so he got his driver's license before the rest of us. On his first solo ride with friends, he took us to the Mapleway roller skating rink in Salt Lake City, where we hoped to pick up girls, and, surprisingly, we did! The girls were all above average and were suitably impressed with the spiffy model A Ford four-door sedan that Dean and his dad had just restored, and that Dean was being allowed to drive for the for the very first time.

Our "Big City Chicks" seemed to like snuggling as much as we did, and Dean's girl nestled right up to him. Suddenly, he pulled over to the curb and shouted at the girls, "Get out!" After they hurriedly did, we asked Dean what the heck he was doing, and was he crazy? He said, "Didn't you see that ninny put her foot up on that dashboard I'd just painted?" Dean was like that.

The plain vanilla Mapleway was an early part of our search-for-girls routine. But as our skating improved, we could take dates to the "Big Berthana" in Ogden without embarrassment. On that huge floor, surrounded by sit-down booths, a humongous rotating mirror ball bathed skaters in moving specks of colored light as they did never ending left turns on a vast hardwood floor. The thundering music of a large theatre organ sped them along. At first, I was partial to "all skate," where I could melt into the pack, but as my skating improved, I joined the holding-hands couples crowd whenever possible. It was all very romantic. But I was a pimply-faced teenager with surging hormones, so everything was.

As any red-blooded American boy—or girl, for that matter—can testify, getting a driver's license as soon as you turn sixteen is a number one priority. The driving portion of my test began at the State Capitol Building in Salt Lake City and wound around the downtown city streets. After a while, the examiner said, "OK, seems like you know this stuff so we can go back a little early." Driving back to the Capitol's parking lot, I kept thinking: *I did it!* As soon as I had skillfully parallel parked the car the examiner said, "You had a near perfect test...until you missed that stop sign turning in here. But you can take the test again next week if you'd like." *Ugggg!*

To date girls, teenage boys in Davis County had to be prepared to drive considerable distances over sometimes-marginal county roads. The usual drill was to take our dates to a movie, a school athletic event, or one of the roller rinks, and then go to a drive-in for food. But if we went to a special church or school dance, where the guys were in suits and the girls in fancy dresses, we'd motor into Salt Lake City to a relatively inexpensive sit-down Chinese restaurant that would always make a fuss over us. To save us embarrassment, the girls would order pork or chicken chow mien because it was the cheapest thing on the menu. By the time you threw in some snuggling (hopefully) and drove everyone home, sometimes in the snow, it was often two or three o'clock in the morning. Remember, this was before airbags and seatbelts of any kind.

My parents had to have had more than a few sleepless nights. But when I was handed the keys to the family car for the first time I was told, "We trust your judgment." After that I never heard a word. This was even more remarkable when you realize that there was only *one* family car. Dad needed that car to commute thirty miles to work in Salt Lake City every weekday, my mother needed it to go grocery shopping and to take us all to church on weekends, and I needed it to go "girling". We all took extremely good care of it.

My only auto accident occurred as I was driving home alone through Centerville late at night, freezing rain pelting down. I suddenly saw a clump of headlight-reflecting deer eyes at the right side of the road, way up ahead, so I slowed to less than fifteen miles per hour. Then, wouldn't you know it, just as I got even with the herd, a large doe bolted out in front of me. I pumped the brakes (what one did before automatic braking) but the car still skidded forward on the ice...*Whump!* The deer was knocked down but immediately got up and ran away. I felt bad enough that I'd hit her, but was devastated when I saw that, even at that slow speed, the collision had cracked the car's chrome grill.

With a heavy heart, I drove our *only* automobile home and went to bed, anxiously tossing and turning until I heard my folks up and about in the morning. I slowly went upstairs to confess my sin and be automatically grounded for years. But before I could get down on my knees and beg for forgiveness, my dad quietly said, "It looks like you hit a deer last night...couldn't have been going very fast...sometimes there's just not much you can do."

That was just like Dad. He could snap at you for seemingly meaningless transgressions, but when you obviously screwed up big, and felt terrible about it, he was calm and philosophical. Nick rolled over the family car, with three other kids inside, trying to negotiate a steep downhill turn on a Farmington Canyon switchback. Dad looked at his badly damaged Chevy, the first new car he had ever owned, and said, "At least he didn't go over the edge (a thousand-foot drop). We'll count our blessings."

Theater Movies were very inexpensive by today's standards, as was the heated, stale popcorn they offered, so we took most girls we dated to the flicks. With or without a date, we preferred to sit in the balcony because we could get away with more up there, including throwing that week-old popcorn at our friends.

Unique to the time was the drive-in-movie. We would load up our car with friends or family, including kids in their jammies, and drive into one of these outdoor movie theaters, parking our car in one of many rows. Through the car's front windshield, we could see the movie projected on a large outdoor screen. Connected to a post on the driver's side was a sturdy window-mounted aluminum-enclosed speaker that provided sound, OK for the time. Every teenager's fantasy was to pile one or two friends into their car's trunk and sneak them into the movie, but I never saw it work.

Our friends, the Walters, took their kids to see *Boxcar Bertha* at the drive-in. Their oldest boy, Larry, supposedly asleep, suddenly exclaimed, "What are they doing to that lady?" "We told him that they were taking off the lady's dress because they wanted to buy her a new one," said Brian. "Then we put the speaker on the pole and quickly drove out of there."

Mom was our moral compass and major motivator. She was a beautiful, bright, unpretentious woman, a counted-on presence, who provided the glue that kept our family together and functioning. She always reminded me that, "Dad always says *no* when you first ask him…until he gets used to it…just let him think about it." Usually worked.

My mom thought about my future when I didn't have a clue and was determined that I'd make something out of myself. The Church was important to her but she didn't press me on it or insist that I go on a church mission. She usually seemed to know the right questions to ask, and frankly, it never occurred to me to outright lie to her… though I might occasionally *massage* the truth a little. I discovered that it was *how* you told Mom things that mattered, and a little humor was usually very helpful. If you got her laughing, you were home free.

Mom gave me two ten-person dress-up candlelight dinner parties while I was in high school, part of her continuing well-meaning program to make me socially acceptable. We used her best, edged-in-gold china and her Chantilly silverware, which I had to correctly place on the tablecloth before the guests arrived. My male guests were expected to wear suits and the women nice dresses (no women's pants suits then). Fortunately, in those days we already had one set of "best clothes" for church and major high school dances. Because my peers knew that the dinners were special events, they watched me to be sure that they were doing the right thing, and I just tried to follow to the letter the instructions Mom and my aunts had given me.

Mom was kind to everyone, even an unlovable old crone, Hattie, who lived in an ancient cabin high on the foothill bench above the cemetery. Occasionally, Hattie would pay Mom an unexpected visit. If she wasn't home, Hattie would just sit on the cold upper step of our concrete front porch, waiting for Mom's return. Hattie had a very loud, high-pitched, gravelly voice, snaggely teeth, and a hump on her back. She usually carried a primitive walking staff, which she would wave and shake like an old-time biblical prophet. She did this whenever she saw frowning Aunt Sue. Theirs was a mutual dislike. They only tolerated each other because they both loved Mom.

But Hattie respected Dad and thought that "Little Bobby" was "cute...but too skinny!" I have to admit that her witch-like persona scared me when I was young, but we became friends as I grew older. Sometimes, I'd even help her carry unusually heavy bags from the Bamberger bus-stop up the half mile of dirt road to her cabin on the foothill bench.

A startling nighttime experience was to encounter Hattie, the self-proclaimed protector of Steed Creek's irrigation water shares, blinding flashlight in one hand, shotgun pointed at me with the other, screaming, "WHAT ARE YOU DOIN' THERE," as I was diverting creek water to our ditch just below her house. "It's just Bobby, Hattie...changing the water." "Oh, Bobby...that's OK then!" She'd lower her shotgun, followed by her flashlight, and we'd have a chat, raucous Hattie's part of which you could hear at our house, far down the hill. When the dialogue started, my folks always knew that things had gone well, so they could stop worrying.

Steed Creek irrigation water passed to our backyard acreage through a long culvert under the lawn. This conduit was a haven for skunks that found some way to survive in spite of poisonous bait, steel traps, and purposely backed-up water, all part of my dad's never-ending war with the odoriferous animals. The skunks were not afraid of the dogs in the neighborhood, including our own, and repeatedly perfumed them. Those frantically barking canines never seemed to get the picture. My brother Pat assures me that Dad eventually got those wily, smelly animals with a shotgun. Maybe, but he couldn't seem to get a decent shot at them while I was living at home. Those canny little critters always seemed to sense what was up and would show him their black and white action-packed backsides as they dove back into the culvert—just ahead of the buckshot.

WORLD WAR II

December 7, 1941 seemed like any other post-church Sunday. I had just begun playing model airplanes with my friend, Paul Buchanan, the local doctor's son, when his worried mom interrupted us: "You better go home now, Bob. Something important has happened and your folks will be worried about you." I slowly walked the mile between downtown Farmington and my home, blithely playing with my B-17 cast-metal model airplane while the whole country sat shocked, glued to their radios, as they absorbed the stunning details of the Japanese sneak attack on Pearl Harbor.

President Roosevelt gave his moving *"...a date that will live in infamy..."* speech the following day, and Congress declared war on Japan, Germany, and Italy. The Country rapidly mobilized and WWII became the biggest thing in our lives. Though I was only eight years old when the war began, I soon learned to identify large numbers of ships and airplanes. We boys would play recess games with flash cards to test our identification skills, but the girls our age only wanted to play nurse. We'd sometimes humor them by pretending to be downed, wounded pilots so they could practice their bandaging.

Out of balsa wood kits and tissue paper, I began building scale models of a few of the most famous allied and enemy planes, and Mom let me hang them from the ceiling of my room. But I saw very few real military aircraft of any kind in the skies over Farmington. The few that did stray over were usually attached to Hill Air Force Base near Ogden. I secretly wished that one or two Japanese warplanes would wander over our house just so I could identify them.

Military camps and airfields sprang up all over. These new facilities needed civilians for support, so, after nearly twelve years of economic depression, unemployed Americans were put back to work, most of them in newly created jobs directly related to the war effort.

For the first time, women were encouraged to work in plants and factories outside the home (symbolized by "Rosie the Riveter" posters) and six million of them did. Women were also welcomed into all branches of the military, where they served as noncombatants, variously known as WAC's, WAVES, WAFS, or WASP's. Though WASP's ferried advanced military aircraft to the war zones, they weren't allowed to fly them into combat as Russian women were. Of course, women nurses were heavily recruited for combat duty in battlefield hospitals and hospital ships. More than 200 army nurses were killed during the war.

It was mind boggling to see what this country could produce for the war effort, and how fast it could ramp up to do it. Agricultural output increased 50%, as we became the world's breadbasket. Twenty million backyard and rooftop "Victory Gardens" produced 40% of the vegetables consumed by us home-front folks. We all did our part and shared with our neighbors.

The United States became the world's arsenal, building unbelievable numbers of tanks, ships, planes, guns, and everything else needed for the war effort. Before the war we were building 300 tanks a year, but after the war began our production rapidly increased to 30,000 per year, which was more than the Germans produced during the whole conflict. Henry Ford's enormous Willow Run plant produced one B24 four-engine bomber every sixty-three minutes. By war's end the United States had produced more than 300,000 military aircraft, 88,000 tanks, 5,800 ships and 40 billion rounds of ammunition. American workers became twice as productive as their German counterparts and five times as productive as Japanese workers.

We were always worried about being bombed or invaded, particularly early in the war when things were going poorly in the Pacific theater. Can you imagine what basket cases we'd have been if we'd had CNN, Fox News, and the other big-hype network news channels then? We'd have probably surrendered! But almost miraculously, six months after Pearl Harbor, our Navy won a decisive victory at the Battle of Midway, a turning point in the Pacific war. Nineteen-forty-three battlefield victories at Guadalcanal and North Africa proved that the Japanese and Germans could be defeated, but at a great cost. We home-front types remained Nervous Nellies until Italy, Germany, and finally Japan surrendered. But fear made it easier for us to put up with the sacrifices required.

Though rumors abounded, the only *real* wartime hostile attacks in or about the Western United States were: the rare torpedoing of ships off our Pacific coast by Japanese submarines; minor submarine shelling episodes in California and Oregon, one each; a single unsuccessful submarine-launched seaplane bombing raid over an Oregon forest; and the release of nine thousand or so small incendiary and antipersonnel bombs ("Fu-Gos") suspended from large hydrogen filled balloons.

The Japanese launched the Fu-Go inflatables from Honshu late in the war, hoping that the jet stream would carry them to the Western United States. Less than one thousand of the non-event weapons (meant to randomly kill and start fires) are thought to have reached the United States and Canada. Most were lost, with little effect, in the mountains and other non-populated areas. Six people who disturbed the remnants of a crashed, unexploded Fu-Go bomb (while on a church outing, of all things) are the only known wartime fatalities caused by these devices. To its credit, the press hushed up reports about any incidents supposedly linked to the balloon-carried bombs, so after a while the Japanese gave up on the program. Very rarely, even today, a hunter or hiker might accidently find a balloon bomb remnant, which they'll hopefully report, because the contraption could still be lethal.

Nearly 16 million men and women served in the armed forces during WWII, at a time when the population of the United States was only 131 million. The Selective Service System, or "draft", furnished 10 million inductees. Fortunately, my Dad was thirty-six years old at the beginning of the war, so he was too old to be drafted, but his younger brother was not so lucky. Uncle Guy was sent to Europe, where shrapnel from a tank shell severely wounded him as he was tending a machine gun during the 1945 Battle of the Bulge. Seventy-five thousand other American servicemen were also wounded or killed during that late war counterattack that represented Hitler's last gasp. Happily, his tanks ran out of gas.

Guy spent the rest of the war in a hospital in England, where they barely succeeded in saving his leg, thanks in part to that new wonder-drug, Penicillin. Uncle Howard Larkins, Beth's husband, was also drafted into the army but was sent to the Pacific theater, where he served unharmed until VJ Day. My mom's half-brother, Ethelbert, flew twin tailed P38 Lockheed "Lightning" fighter planes in the Pacific area until the war was over. Considering that over 400 thousand servicemen lost their lives during the war, our family got off easy.

When Uncle Howard came home he gave me a folding Japanese pistol, which my mom promptly confiscated, and a fur-lined leather Japanese aviator helmet (so small I couldn't wear it) that she let me keep. I did get some helmet mileage at our school's brand of show-and-tell, but the pistol would have been better.

For almost four years, the war effort dramatically affected our lives. Our gas and food was rationed, but my Dad commuted to work at a public utility in Salt Lake City, so he had different gas ration stamps and windshield decal colors than most Farmington residents. This allowed him to get considerably more gas, and even new car tires, when needed.

We ate very little meat because most of it was being sent to the troops. Butter was replaced by greasy white margarine that we could turn faux-butter yellow by kneading a broken orange dye capsule into an oily white brick of trans fat. We did raise a few chickens for their eggs and would eat one of those birds when we could spare it. Commercial produce was scarce, but our large Victory Garden allowed us to can most of our vegetables and fruit. The government suggested that people give $18.75 War Bonds (worth $25.00 after ten years) for Christmas and birthday gifts, and some did. Boy, how we kids hated that.

Because the military got the vast majority of the new tires produced, recapping with non-rationed recycled rubber was a booming concern. Dad worked many weekends in a recap shop. This was in part to help the war effort, filling in for those who were in the service, but it was also because we needed the money. For the same two reasons, he even helped empty boxcars, until his back gave out. Recognition of how hard he worked, often exposed to the winter elements, became a great motivator for me in high school and college.

Even with the war on, my folks were somehow able to obtain two small fleets of navy ship models made out plastic. If we floated these hollow flat bottom vessels on the goldfish pond, they all listed to port or starboard, as if they were sinking, so we had to stage our plastic navy battles on a floor or sidewalk.

These dry-land sea battles soon bored Johnny Koroulis and me, so we built our own small wooden ships that would float upright on my dad's lily-pad laden fishpond till we bombed or torpedoed them. Once, when the pond was empty for cleaning, we tried floating our fleet on some dammed-up septic tank effluent we found trickling down a steep embankment on the Neumann's side of our property line. To us, it didn't smell much different than the lily-pond water did just before Dad cleaned it. Both organic, I suppose.

By nailing together two scrap boards perpendicular to each other, and attaching two old roller skates to the bottom, Johnny and I made fighter planes we could kneel on and ride like scooters on the road...just out of Mom's sight. We could roughly steer these crude craft by pushing a wing down hard to the ground in the direction we wanted to turn. Before our military activities were discovered, we both scooted a mile into town on our creations and tried them out on sidewalks. That free-lance sortie earned us brig time and our aircraft were impounded and dismantled. It's a wonder that a car didn't take us out while we were flying missions on those things.

Obviously, we kids needed personal protection from the Japanese in case they did invade, so with scrap boards, we built an elaborate two level fort in the thick spreading branches of an old box elder tree and dug foxholes around its base. We learned to make a "rubber gun" using a grip-mounted clothespin that secured the near end of a rubber band (cut from old inner tube) that we stretched out to the muzzle. These elastic projectiles could fly up to twenty-five feet when released. We even devised a rudimentary wooden machine gun variant by stretching rubber bands from the muzzle to notches along the upper edge of the gun's breech, so we could launch the projectiles with a pull of a trip string. That creative weapon gave us considerably more firepower.

We had impressive war games. Abandoned chicken coops were great for urban warfare and the cemetery was a particularly good fighting field. Sunken graves (caused by rotten and caved in caskets) were ready-made foxholes and upright headstones (some of humongous size) provided fine cover. As much as I liked playing war, it's good that real hostilities ended in September of 1945, before I was old enough to sneak into the military and get killed—or worse.

While the war was going on, mother's three sisters, Sue, Betty, and Dora, and all of their kids, descended on us from Texas and California, all planning to put up fruits and vegetables with my mom during their summer visit. Ten extra people stayed with us for a large chunk of the summer, much to the dismay of my dad, who liked his privacy. But we kids loved it!

We worked and played all over the neighboring vegetable fields, orchards, foothills, and the cemetery across the street. We slept side by side on cots in the basement—when we weren't telling ghost stories in the dark and scaring the bejesus out of ourselves. We put on frequent skits and musical extravaganzas, usually war-inspired. Exaggerated characterizations of Hitler, Tojo, and Mussolini often showed up in our productions, as did Spike Jones and the City Slickers' peppy ballad "Der

Fuehrer's Face", silly comedic relief that we sang and marched to and included in our skits. That summer was a much-needed interlude.

Model airplane building became my passion as the war progressed. Using an X-Acto knife, I'd carefully cut out airplane parts and stringers from printed balsa wood sheets, pin them on a pattern, glue them together to make a plane's airframe, and then cover that skeleton with glued-on tissue paper that would shrink tight when wet. A suitable "dope" (paint) color was brushed on the dried airplane skin before I added appropriate military insignia and decoration. After winding up their internal rubber band motors, I'd fly some of those creations, always wishing that I could afford to buy a hard-to-come-by *real* gas motor. But I might as well have wished for machine guns.

Near the end of the war, our ward scoutmaster bought a real war surplus glider— similar to those used in the D-Day invasion—and invited us newer scouts over to play in it. We took turns manning the two *real* steering columns and the crude machine guns we'd built out of wood. It was a heavy bomber to us and we did considerable damage to the Germans ("Krauts") or Japanese ("Japs") on our missions. Sometimes, one of our crewmembers would get badly wounded, or even killed, but we'd fix him up so he could be on the next raid. We used that quick fix in all of our war games because no one wanted to stay dead—unless he had to go home anyway.

Throughout the war, music made things seem a little better, as it does now, but recordings were not easy to come by. Aunt Beth had a 78-RPM record changer and we didn't, so I jumped at the chance to baby-sit Beth's kids. I'd stack on "Chattanooga Choo Choo,"[2] "Boogie Woogie Bugle Boy,"[3] "The White Cliffs Of Dover,"[4] "Don't Sit Under The Apple Tree,"[5] "Praise The Lord And Pass The Ammunition,"[6] and "White

---

[2] The Glen Miller orchestra, 1941.
[3] The Andrew Sisters, 1941.
[4] Vera Lynn, 1942.
[5] The Andrews Sisters, 1942.
[6] Kay Kyser, 1942.

Christmas,"[7] just a few of the songs that became instantly popular as millions of "Our Boys" went off to war and lives were put on hold, or for many…*on end.*

As the war slogged on, I added to the spindle-stack: "Paper Doll,"[8] "I'll Be Seeing You,"[9] "You'd Be So Nice to Come Home To,"[10] "Have Yourself A Merry Little Christmas,"[11] and "Long ago and Far Away".[12] These songs resonated with all us war weary folks. (You Tube has almost all of these songs in movie segments, some from the films they first appeared in.)

We seldom missed a WWII movie. We usually had to go to Bountiful to see the first-run films, most of them in black and white, but Dwain Bybee might eventually show the good ones on Movie Night. *Mrs. Minever*[13] was an academy award-winning film about the British home front during the Battle of Britain in 1940. It was a favorite of Mom's, so I got to see this tearjerker at least three times during the war. *Flying Tigers*[14] was a crowd favorite that had American mercenaries flying old P40 fighter planes— tiger mouths painted on their engine air-intake cowlings—slugging it out with Japanese aviators over China before our declared war had begun. *Wake Island*[15] got our juices going as we saw the Japanese pummel our boys until the hated enemy finally conquered the island. This was a good recruiting film. *Casablanca*[16] was another academy award winner set in North Africa in the early days of the war, a *must* see then and now. *Guadalcanal Diary*[17] made us feel better because it reminded us that we were finally fighting back and winning. *Thirty Seconds Over Tokyo*[18] dramatized—with lots of newsreel footage—Jimmy Doolittle's aircraft carrier-launched, one-way, B25 bombing raid over Tokyo in 1942. That early token payback for Pearl Harbor made us proud, though by the time that film was released, in 1944, our B29s were bombing Japan regularly.

---

[7] Bing Crosby, 1942.
[8] The Mills Brothers, 1943.
[9] Bing Crosby, 1944.
[10] Dinah Shore, 1943.
[11] Judy Garland, 1944.
[12] Gene Kelly and Rita Hayworth, 1944.
[13] Greer Garson and Walter Pidgeon, 1942.
[14] John Wayne, 1942.
[15] Brian Donlevy, Robert Preston, and William Bendix, 1942.
[16] Humphrey Bogart and Ingrid Bergman, 1943.
[17] Preston Foster, Lloyd Nolan and William Bendix, 1943.
[18] Van Johnson, Spencer Tracy, Robert Mitchum, and Robert Walker, 1944.

These are just a few of the many movies that kept us going during those WWII days. Granted, it was usually easy to tell the good guys from bad, but that was the way we liked it. Make no mistake—they *were* bad guys! Many fine movies about the war have been made since VJ Day, and good films are continuing to be made, a few emphasizing the Holocaust. Wikipedia has an exhaustive, continually updated "List of World War II Films". Some are excellent.

The two-part end to WWII (Italy had already surrendered in 1943) began May 8th, 1945, when Nazi Germany unconditionally surrendered (V-E Day). News reels showed Soldiers and Sailors hugging and kissing good-looking girls in New York's Times Square to celebrate the event. Three months and two atom bomb explosions—hopefully saving millions of lives—later, Japan also surrendered (VJ Day). Again, soldiers and sailors were kissing pretty girls in Times Square, but everyone was kissing everyone, everywhere. I was twelve...I kissed my Mom.

At the dedication of the World War II Memorial in Washington, DC, it was noted: "...The war made heroes of farm and city boys, many just kids...Farm boys, who had never flown before, learned to fly massive four engine bombers and teenagers became sergeants...Their lives were interrupted; their futures forever altered; their dreams were held in stasis; every minute of youth was burdened with fear, with loss and with uncertainty. Lest we forget."

Please watch the outstanding PBS miniseries "*The War*," by Ken Burns to see how we mobilized and sacrificed, some much more than others, to win WWII. If you're in Washington DC, the World War II Memorial is a must, as is the United States Holocaust Museum. Of course, in Hawaii the USS Arizona Memorial in Pearl Harbor is a must see. "Remember Pearl Harbor!" was our slogan throughout the war—and still should be.

SCOUT BOB

Our Boy Scout troop was definitely a low budget operation. There was a lot of war surplus hiking and camping material available after VJ day, so we got reasonably well outfitted on the cheap. But the wide berth we gave to the pricier Boy Scouts of America gear gave us a ragtag appearance at scout jamborees…like a guerrilla army of mountain men.

"Life is a journey, not a destination," wrote Ralph Waldo Emerson. Well, going to our scout camp qualified as both. After we piled into the back of our scoutmaster's old one-ton flatbed truck, with plywood sides and hay bales to sit on, we bounced ourselves silly all the way to Camp Stiner. That bumpy ride to and from camp was a free-for-all. We'd stand up against the cab, sing, shout, wave to people, and wrestle and tumble about until we were bruised, could hardly talk, and our eyelids turned sore and puffy from windburn. No one had heard of liability in those days. That threat would have kept us poorly financed irregulars at home for sure.

I saw jagged mountain peaks, carpets of evergreen trees, and crystal-clear lakes, heard gurgling streams and roaring waterfalls, and smelled fresh alpine scents in those high Uinta Mountains. We'd hike, fish, and swim, ending each day around a crackling campfire, cooking our dinner, eating, singing, and telling ghost stories. Some kids got homesick and had to have their parents come pick them up early—but not old Scout Bob! They'd have to conduct an organized search for me when it was time to go home.

Hiking was exhilarating in that spectacular mountain country—a religious experience far exceeding any church testimony meeting, I'll tell you. But a cloudy day climb to Hayden Peak (elevation 12,476 ft.) was almost my last act on earth.

I was part of a leaderless pack of five scouts that had separated from the main hiking group in hopes of making it to the top first. Near the peak, we were climbing on a four-foot-wide crest-trail, flanked on both sides by cliffs and slopes of debris that dropped steeply to valleys far below. I noticed that the hair of the redheaded kid in front of me was standing straight up and we both laughed about it. We were smart enough to know that this was probably static electricity, but not wise enough to know what might follow—so we kept on climbing

We had just begun our descent from the peak (*alone,* we soon realized) when a bolt of lightning danced on the crest-trail three hundred yards ahead of us, and a deafening clap of thunder almost blew us off the path. Like startled deer, we jumped over the side and slid and tumbled down the scree-covered slope to the relative safety of the stunted fir and scrub below. We watched in awe as a terrifying lightning and thunder show erupted above us. Bruised but alive, we rejoined the troop and all said a short prayer, the least we could do.

As tradition demanded, each Thanksgiving morning our scout troop met at the Lagoon resort to practice our wood cutting skills. Then, with scouts riding shotgun, the product was piled high into two or three trucks and delivered to the town's widows to help them cook their Thanksgiving dinners. The women always seemed glad to see us and would give us a cookie, some candy, or a hot drink. I'm sure that most of those ladies probably cooked with gas or electricity by then, but the custom was such a pleasurable event for everyone (at least that's what *we* thought) that the troop kept it going. After my dad died, Mom said that she realized she really was a widow when the scouts brought her wood. She burned hers in the fireplace at Christmas.

I loved that faux-military scout stuff: the three-fingered saluting, the showy award ceremonies, and the medals (merit badges). They didn't just *give* those little patches away in our troop. They expected months of effort for each one, so it was a long time to before I really looked cool. School interests and girls eventually superseded my merit badge quest, so I stopped scouting just shy of my Eagle award. But hey, I learned a surprising number of things and had a great time scouting. My scout-mates and I were certainly mutually improved, which was the intent, I suppose.

YOUNG BOB AT WORK

Mom ran a childhood sweatshop in the summer She was determined that I would learn to work at an early age, so she was always on the lookout for a new employment opportunity for me. And in that small rural farming community, she had no trouble finding it. I complained a lot, but soon admitted that it was nice to have my own discretionary income.

I began working for our Greek farmer neighbor, Louis Mehas, when I was eight years old. He had me weeding and harvesting his beets, carrots, radishes, onions, corn and melons and paid me fifty cents a day. My union boss mother decided that the wage was too low, even for those days, so some tough bargaining began. During negotiations, she learned that I often stared into space and cut out, or otherwise destroyed, some of the vegetable plants I was supposedly nurturing. But Mr. Mehas grudgingly agreed to double my salary and make it equal that of his stepson, my buddy Johnny Koroulis, whom he also considered a work in progress.

I eventually found that little bit of extra money indispensable; I could no longer be denied a comic book I craved or a cheap little treasure I yearned for at Kress. And when a Wheaties Decoder Ring or an Ovaltine pedometer became available on a radio program, I could buy it. I even had enough left over to start a savings account at the Davis County Bank and get my own bankbook, to bankroll future splurges. That's how capitalists are created.

After the onset of WWII, there were no men available to tend the cemetery grounds, so our family became temporary graveyard custodians. Those were four tough temporary years as we hauled hoses and sprinklers, cut the vast lawn area with a heavy old gas-powered mower, and edged around hundreds of erect headstones by hand. But the worst part of the job was dealing with the small salamanders, and pieces of salamanders, that squeezed through the main reservoir's outlet screens and plugged up the cemetery's water sprinklers. These had to be taken apart and cleaned by hand, and the sprinkler nozzles blown out by mouth—*I can still taste it!*

Tending the cemetery did provide some lighter moments. We repeatedly caught and displayed a fearless six-foot long blow snake that would hiss on cue when shown to friends. A large tarantula I'd captured while mowing the cemetery was also a hit. Artfully done, a specter's nighttime rise from a sunken grave could be truly frightening for gaggles of flashlight-carrying girls we'd sometimes lure to South Farmington to see our unnerving act. They'd always humor us with a bloodcurdling scream or two, even if they'd seen it all before.

Because there were no obstructing headstones on the lower part of the cemetery lawn, a solitary streetlight allowed us to play nighttime football using a white painted ball. A defensive advantage for either team was that you were likely to run into an unseen upright headstone, or a box elder tree, if you ran too far away from the lamppost, making the offense more predictable. I always tried to be on Bruno Newman's team. Bruno was twice the size of the rest of us, so his team always had the best running game. If you were playing offense against Bruno, you had to be able to get rid of that white ball fast when the big guy was blitzing—an anxiety producer for sure.

When we stopped being cemetery custodians, I became a summer fruit-picker in the surrounding orchards. First came the cherries, followed by the apricots, then the peaches, and lastly the grapes. Good money could be made picking fruit, if you applied yourself, so each morning I would attack the fruit tree ladder with a renewed determination to concentrate and make some of that big money. But once picking began, I would notice a double-headed dragonfly, a spider-web with a striped spider on it, a nest of baby birds, or some other wonder of nature, and my mind would begin to wander. Soon it was: *one for the bucket...one for me...one for the bucket....* But I picked enough to keep my job. I didn't want to face Mom with a pink slip (firing notice, in my day).

Near the end of WWII, we worked alongside some German prisoners of war who were bussed in each day to help us pick fruit while the folks in Washington DC tried to decide what to do with them. They were friendly guys and wanted to learn English before they went home, so we "chewed the fat" (one of many slang phrases we taught them) on our breaks. Using a common ladle, we all drank water from a big stainless steel milk can that contained a floating chunk of ice. Not too sanitary, but it was really cool to be drinking "Wasser" with the enemy. There was no doubt that these former goose-stepping soldiers of the Wehrmacht were grateful to have been captured by us Americans and *not* the Russians.

Gunter Newman hired me to work on his dairy farm one summer. Gunter had two dogs: a big, white, lovable Old English Sheepdog named Whiskers, and a nasty black Doberman, appropriately named Blitzkrieg. The Doberman was a snarling creature that Gunter kept tied up on his rickety front porch, but the sheepdog was a working member of the family. Whiskers would round up the cows, open and close the pasture gates, put the cows in their correct stalls, and take them back out to the fields after milking. At lunchtime, the dog would perform tricks for us as he balanced on a high plank in the barn. Frankly, he was smarter than Gunter.

The Doberman would often growl and lunge at me, but his chain always brought him up short—except for one terrifying time when his tether snapped as he leapt. I dropped to the ground, hands behind my neck, fearing that I'd bought the farm, so to speak. Suddenly, there was a flash of white, a snarling, growling cacophony, and a tumbling mass. A bloody, yelping Blitzkrieg emerged from the melee and hobbled toward the house, Whiskers nipping at his heels. After hugging and thanking my canine superhero, I rewarded him with his favorite thing: "Whiskers...let's go get the cows." His limp disappeared as he raced for the gate.

A *Deseret News* afternoon paper route was my punishment for turning twelve. It was my ball and chain for four long years. Big cities had wussy sidewalk routes where a guy could toss seventy to eighty papers in forty-five minutes, walking or biking. But my afternoon up and downhill rural slog was nearly four miles long, so it took me two to three hours of serious after-school bike riding to deliver a measly forty or fifty papers, sun, rain, sleet, or snow.

Some parts weren't so bad; I liked riding my bike and chatting with people, and there was the money, of course. But folding and tossing that same meager paper load day after day took me out of most afternoon action with my friends, and that wore on me over time. But by far the most distasteful part of being a paperboy was collecting the money each month. Can you believe that a few of those good "Saints" actually tried to stiff the paperboy? I'll bet they didn't try that with God and their tithing.

The last family on my paper route lived in a railroad-owned house adjacent to the Union Pacific train station. Now and again, these gracious folks would invite me in for some lemonade or cocoa because they knew I'd delivered my last paper for the day. A sixteen-wheel steam locomotive might roar by while we were talking, the deafening whistle and the rumbling *click clack, click clack* of its long string of cars stopping all conversation. We'd stare at each other...at the floor...or out the window until the caboose passed by. Then, as if starting from "pause" on a DVD player, a seamless discussion of the previous topic would resume. "Doesn't that train bother you?" I once asked my host. "What train?" he answered, incredulous.

The words of a transiently popular mid-fifties song[19] seem appropriate: "The railroad comes through the middle of the house—it comes and goes through the middle of the house—but we don't live in the middle house—cause that's the railroad track." You can see that music was much simpler in my day.

After four long years, high school wrestling, speech, and drama activities finally earned me a pardon from *Deseret News* prison. My folks had been great about helping me deliver papers in really bad storms, or when I was sick, but once they got a steady diet of being my substitute carrier, the job abruptly ended, and modest winter allowances supplemented my summer savings.

The last summer before I turned sixteen and could work at Lagoon amusement park, I slaved at Farmington's only other major corporate entity, the Miller Floral Company ("A Quarter of a Million Feet of Glass"). No matter where you were in Farmington

---

[19] "In the middle of the house (1956)," Rusty Draper or Vaughn Monroe.

at noontime, the Floral's shrill, piercing steam whistle seemed to ask: How's your day going thus far? The five-o'clock blast queried: "Did it end any better?"

Unfortunately, I was too young to work on the Floral's shovel gang, a sought-after job scooping dirt and cow manure into greenhouse flower beds amid the bawdy camaraderie of super-cool and heavily muscled high school guys. Most of the gang members were hoping to work for the large wholesale florist for the rest of their lives, a career path that never crossed my mind.

Alas, I was relegated to the ignoble task of watering the roses—pulling long hoses up and down the paths between elevated beds of rose bushes, stiflingly enclosed in glass "hot houses" (aptly named). The jungle-like milieu helped me think about a lot of things that summer, not the least of which was what I needed to do to ensure that the Miller Floral Company did *not* become my future. But I learned to whistle like a pro in those muggy echo chambers. Lowell Hess said that I was the only guy he had ever heard who could whistle a tune and accompany himself.

After the war, Uncle Howard drove a delivery truck for Hod Sanders Potato Chips. His job seemed pretty cool, something I might like to do instead of going to college, so I was really excited when he took me with him to deliver chips and snacks to stores on his Bingham Canyon route. At Bingham City's Overlook we stopped for lunch, which included (you guessed it) a big freshly opened bag of those tasty Hod Sanders chips. We peered into the maw of the gigantic Kennecott open pit copper mine, the largest in the world at the time, as a chunk of the lower crater wall peeled away in a puff of smoke from a dynamite explosion way down in the pit. Soon, seemingly tiny but really huge loaders were filling gigantic dump trucks with ore that was to be hauled up out of the mine and taken to the smelter.

"This town's days are numbered, Bob," said Uncle Howard. "Where we're sitting will just be air." Sure enough, in 1971 they tore down the entire town to expand the mine. When I now look at the excavation from the air, I try to estimate just where above that pit we were eating our lunch that day. Then I have another chip...*Hod Sanders tasted better, Uncle Howard.*

Uncle Howard was a cowboy at heart and had herded cattle on his family's ranch, but he was also into farming. So, when he got back from the war he bought Grandma's place next door—with Grandma still in it—and talked Dad into sharing their combined three acres to grow garden crops and alfalfa for hay. They soon purchased a milk cow and a few pigs. Together with the chickens we'd begun raising during WWII, we had quite the little farm.

Unfortunately, even small farms require considerable work, which Uncle Howard and Dad seemed to enjoy, so maybe Bob would too? Uncle Howard volunteered to teach me how to milk a cow so I could take part in the five AM milking rotations, but he soon complained, "That kid is not teachable, Alton." *You got that right, Uncle Howard!*

I made sure that my pig farming skills were sub-par as well. But I couldn't fool Mom when it came to chicken tending, even if I dropped a few eggs. "Don't kid me, Bob! Anyone can carefully gather eggs and clean out under the roost. And *so— can—you!*" (repeated finger points for emphasis).

I gathered eggs, and tried to be a sport about it, but a few of the old hens pecked my hand when I reached under them, so I was not unhappy when one of these was selected for stewing. I never volunteered to be the chicken executioner, but I didn't shrink from that responsibility, if asked. I'd pull on my black hood (just kidding, kids) and try to cleanly cut off the condemned bird's head with my first hatchet blow, not an easy task with all that wing flapping.

Grandma, a long-time member of the chicken executioner's local, suggested that I stroke a finger down the bird's outstretched neck. For some strange reason, this seemed to magically hypnotize and immobilize the avian creature. That made my *fowl* task much easier, though the occasional sight of a chicken's headless body running around spurting blood from its carotid arteries always bothered me. But we had to eat, and chicken meat didn't come in a package.

LAGOON

In 1896, Simon Bamberger drained a swamp north of Farmington and built a resort
adjacent to his steam (later electric) train railroad track. Later improvements gave
the folks from Salt Lake City and Ogden one of the finest resorts in the west. They
could now swim in fresh filtered water ("Water Fit to Drink") instead of the foul-
smelling Great Salt Lake or hot springs liquids they'd dipped in previously.

When I began working at Lagoon, in 1949, the park boasted a man-made lake (a
"lagoon" by loose definition) that had a scaled-down steam engine train ride chugging
around it and rented rowboats splashing to and fro. Swimmers of all ages flocked to

the park's large, newly rebuilt outdoor swimming and diving areas, unequaled anywhere in the country at the time.

Part owner Ranch Kimball, a well-known commercial artist, had created modern, eye-pleasing building decorations throughout the park, harmonizing games, rides, and food stands with strikingly beautiful midway flower gardens. Lagoon's famous master gardener artist, Carl Stayner, planted new creations each spring, using exotic plants grown in the parks greenhouses. For two spring seasons, I helped master Carl plant the flowers in those gardens. I should have paid more attention...and whistled less.

Several park attractions were architectural relics of the late nineteenth and early twentieth century: a gigantic wooden roller coaster (by John Miller of Coney Island fame); a unique Fun House; an open air dance pavilion with twinkling star-lights shining down from overhead ceiling trusses and a raised big band stage; an 1893 vintage merry-go-round with wood-carved animals and real Wurlitzer music; and several various-sized covered, open-air picnic boweries where just a few, or a few hundred, people could meet, eat, mingle, put on stage shows, enjoy the adjacent lawns and trees, and take in the nearby midway excitement. The dance hall and the boweries had been moved from Lake Park, which had previously existed on the now far away shores of a receding Great Salt Lake.

Midway attractions were what people came for, starting with a Fun House that advertised: two large end-to-end, counter-rotating, oak-lined barrels in which you could walk, tumble, or do spread-eagled three-sixties (if you were tall and strong enough); a large rotating floor saucer that used centrifugal force to hurl a huddled clump of sitting, resisting people to a padded periphery; a three-story oak slippery-slide on which revelers, three abreast on gunny sacks, could scoot to the bottom while holding hands; tilting and undulating floor sections; and all forms of image-distorting mirrors. But the Fun House piece de resistance was a network of hidden holes in the floor from which an operator, controlling jets of compressed air, could randomly startle people or blow up women's skirts. In those days, women wore skirts to places like that...hard to imagine now.

Modern amusement park rides were clustered around one end of the midway: the Flying Scooters swung several two-person, cable-suspended cars out from a rotating center post, allowing riders to control their flight by large vertical front airfoils—great for after-hours water balloon fights with squirt-gun toting rowboat attendants on the ground below; the Dodgem bumper cars allowed drivers to plow into each other hoping to produce whiplash or worse; the Hammer wildly rotated people in two opposing pods that you didn't want to stand under because its centrifugally forced passengers often got sick; and the Rockets (identical to the Golden Zephyr ride in Disney's California Land) orbited multiple riders in cable-suspended, rocket-shaped cars out over the lake and park for a birds-eye view.

Newer children's rides were scattered about the end of the midway but, these were pretty lame, so I never volunteered to work in them.

A large variety of food and drink concessions lined the midway, as did many fancy amusement park games. My favorite was the shooting gallery that used real pump 22 rifles and 22 short bullets to knock down moving steel targets and ring bells. With skill, concentration, and considerable luck, a shooter could win gaudy prizes, including stuffed animals of immense size. The decades-old gallery had an accumulation of lead dust that often became airborne in the wind. I still think about that circulating toxin when I have memory issues.

The penny arcade had a penny-a-play "How much electricity can you take?" shocker contraption. The bright-red eyes of an upright-sitting ceramic pig would light up if you could withstand the maximum electrical jolt…and so would yours. A shuffle card peep show, a grip strength device, and a fortune-teller machine—from the really old days—sat alongside pinball machines, claw prize devices, and a photo gallery. No video stuff then.

My first Lagoon job was to help open the big new outdoor swimming pool complex. I checked men's clothes in wire baskets, provided towels, and joked and talked my head off with the hundreds of friendly folks on holiday. Naturally gregarious, I was in my element and happy as that proverbial mollusk. At the end of the day, I'd volunteer for extra work, paid or not, take a free swim, and then cruise the park to check in with my staff-mates. Like me, most of Lagoon's employees were high school or college students working for the summer.

I'd worked in the Swim less than a month when Bob Freed, the park's co-owner/manager, called me in to tell me that he'd noticed my "infectious enthusiasm" and he'd like me to be the new salaried Excursion Manager. I'd have done it free.

Within days, I was stapling up large, professionally painted paper signs on the boweries, welcoming: Zion Bank, Salt Lake 21st Ward, Ogden School District, BYU Class of 31, and so on. I'd be there at dawn, rolling out clean white butcher paper on the picnic tables, getting out and testing the loud speaker systems, making sure that the large wheeled tubs of iced pop and beer arrived on time, and coordinating all major park excursion events. In addition to my modest salary (less than I would have made working equivalent hours at the Swim), I got to wear a Lagoon T-shirt, carry a large official-looking clipboard, and meet many more girls than if I'd still been working in the Swim's men's locker room.

Lagoon was even more magical at night when the lights came on. I would sometimes stick around after I'd finished my picnic duties and fill in for the people who worked on the games, rides, and in the dancehall. Occasionally, I even got to blow up skirts in the Fun House. I never volunteered for the food-stands—no prestige there. *Real* status was substituting for the roller coaster guys. I could give cute girls extra rides when crowds were light. The Beach Boys specifically mention Lagoon's "...cutest in the western states..." girls in their "Salt Lake City" song lyrics.

My favorite fill-in was the dancehall. Because I was a wrestler, they let me try bouncer team relief, but at one hundred and forty pounds, I was bluffing. A drunken patron with a broken beer bottle made me rethink things: *Maybe I should just take tickets, stamp hands, and help with the big bands...thank you very much.* In fact, I was a three-night gofer for "Spike Jones and the City Slickers," a zany, two-hour long musical spectacular. Spike's show was the biggest thing going in my day. After the group's last performance, Spike personally gave me a program signed by the entire cast and a fifty-dollar bill, a big tip for those days.

Though I was hardly a chick magnet, for the better part of a summer I true-loved a comely lass from Salt Lake City whom I'd met at the park. Bonnie's dad drove a bus for Greyhound, which I thought was cool. After work, I would call her on one of Lagoon's ten pay phones. I knew all of Farmington's telephone operators, so, after I deposited ten cents, they'd usually let me talk to Bonnie long distance for a while...sometimes for up to an hour. But if they were especially busy, the operators would break in and say, "We've got a paying customer, Bob. We need the line."

I commuted two miles to work on a heavy old underpowered Cushman motor scooter, which had one of the first automatic transmissions. I had to give it a strong push to get it going and provide some additional help on even just a moderate grade, but once it was moving on the flat straightaway it could motor along at about 35 miles per hour.

Scootering home from Lagoon at cruising speed, I was often chased by a large, barking dog. Boris would intercept me and run alongside the scooter, trying to bite off my right lower leg. I would swing both legs to the left as I passed him, resulting in a balancing act second only to Chinese acrobats.

But one day old Boris misjudged the pattern and I hit him square on. I'll never know how I kept from going down, but I eventually controlled my two-wheeled machine and, after observing that my attacker was not only down but immobile, circled back to check on him.

As I putt-putted up to the cur, he popped open one eye, painfully got up, and limped off yelping. The Boris problem was solved. Though he might still lie in wait at the side of the road for an unsuspecting bicyclist, he would invariably yelp and streak for the house when he heard that Cushman coming.

Unfortunately, I ceased being part of Lagoon's magic when I entered college and began taking summer training cruises with the navy. In the short time available between the end of each cruise and the start of school I had to make *big* money, so I lived at home and worked on the first freeway being built through Davis County.

I was still living at home, in 1953, when Lagoon's grand old dancehall, the Fun House, and part of the rollercoaster burned to the ground. The inferno was the most spectacular thing Farmington had ever seen. Though the dance hall was immediately replaced with a large modern venue in another location, and the Fun House and rollercoaster were restored, the park never seemed quite the same after that. Lagoon and I moved on. Bob Freed never forgot me. In fact, his exceptional reference letter helped me get into medical school later on.

But before I leave the Lagoon subject, let me relate two vignettes about Hugh Roberts, my then-seventy-four-year-old grandpa, who was also employed by Lagoon for a while—as a night watchman, of all things. You can see that park security was a low priority

"Grandpa Hughie," as the staff affectionately called him, only carried a few keys and a flashlight, so he was obviously not expected to shoot it out with bandits. For that we had the Davis County Sheriff, whom my grandfather was supposed to call if he saw anything suspicious. Unfortunately, on his nightly rounds one evening three masked bandits, who had obviously cased the joint, suddenly confronted him. Their leader politely said, "Dad, take these handcuffs and cuff yourself to that desk leg," which he quickly did. Then they trussed him up and taped over his eyes. After the crooks had blown the safe, and tossed the place in general, they came back and asked Grandpa if there was anything they might have missed…information he cheerfully provided. The burglars got away and Gramps stayed tied up until morning.

Grandpa Hugh was quite the celebrity after that. Salt Lake City's two newspapers, the *Deseret News* and the *Salt Lake Tribune*, quoted his comments about the robbery. The following week's edition of the *Davis County Clipper* also had a big spread about the incident. My Mom was the Clipper's Farmington reporter, so her scoop was more detailed, but Grandpa probably embellished his story after he'd had more time to think about it. He loved being a celebrity.

SALT LAKE CITY, UTAH,

THURSDAY, JULY 6, 1950

Police Grope For Clue in Lagoon Job

Speedy Thieves Escape With $21,000 in Loot

By WILLIAM B. SMART

Investigators Thursday were without a clue in what shaped up as one of the biggest robberies in Utah's history.

Officials of Lagoon resort finally settled on a figure of $21,342.20 as the loot two armed, masked robbers carried away, apparently in a gunny sack.

It was the entire take of the four-day Fourth of July holiday, plus a "cash reserve." It was in small bills and in "pennies, nickels and dimes," Robert E. Freed, resort manager, said.

The money sacked up in at least 14 cash bags, ready for the bank. The two gunmen would have had to make several trips to their car with their loot unless they used a large gunny sack.

IT HAPPENED TOO FAST

Hugh Roberts, left, elderly nightwatchman at Lagoon resort, was unable to identify any suspects Thursday as he looked through picture files of criminals at Salt Lake City police headquarters. The bandits were masked and he had little time to watch them, he explained.

Grandpa always took the initiative, but that proved to be his downfall at Lagoon. In the early spring, while the Park was still closed, Gramps got bored and began looking around for some real work. He decided that many of the park's shrubs and small trees were out of control and needed to be pruned. Well, my grandfather never did anything in a small way, so by the time anyone noticed, he had severely cut back most of the bushes and many of the small trees. When Bob Freed asked Grandpa why he'd carried it to the extreme, he replied that, in his experience, occasional severe pruning was good for most bushes and that everything would look "first rate by fall." "But Hugh—by then we'll be closed!"

OLD HILLTOP

Virtually everyone living in Farmington had attended our aging elementary school, "Old Hilltop." It's probable that my first grade teacher, Edith Walsh, had taught the school's very first class. Miss Walsh was an austere, no-nonsense spinster who wore no makeup, peered through wire rimmed glasses, pulled her hair back in a tight bun, and took no prisoners...except in my case. She somehow got the idea that I had a deportment problem, so she covered my mouth with scotch tape and sat me on a chair in our room's supply closet. She made two mistakes: she didn't tie me up, and she forgot that the light switch was on my side of the door. When my jail time was up, I usually had the supplies organized and was beginning the art period early. She must have liked my work in the closet because I ended up there quite frequently, always with my mouth taped shut.

Believe it or not, in spite of those repeated incarcerations, I liked the fearsome Miss Walsh. But I *loved* Mrs. Sessions, my second grade teacher. She was a handsome woman with a soft voice and a melt-a-boy smile. I often raised my hand to complain that I couldn't hear her, hoping that would get me moved closer to her desk. When that didn't happen, I had to once again use the deportment card. That always worked.

I made a major discovery in the second grade. As part of my trip to the bathroom, I could explore the building and grounds for short periods of time. I'm sure that Mrs. Sessions thought that I had the smallest bladder in the school, but she never refused me. Unfortunately, this only worked in the second grade. After I'd been hauled back to class two or three times in the third grade, the word was out. Though I can't remember much about my third grade teacher, I know that she became inflexible. A restroom visit at recess had to become part of my busy schedule.

My fourth grade teacher, Miss Huber, was plump, hirsute (had a mustache as prominent as mine is now), had a large purple mole on her left cheek, wore her hair back in a tight bun, and was very strict. Unfortunately, I can remember little else about her or the fourth grade.

John Walsh, my fifth grade teacher and Edith's brother, was also formidable. In addition to having the worst halitosis I've ever encountered, he had a bad habit of sneaking up on you from the back of the room and loudly smacking your desk with a large oak ruler. You always had to know where Mr. Walsh was, which certainly hindered the learning process.

Mr. Knowlton, the school principal, also taught the sixth grade. Above the blackboard on the wall behind his desk was a big picture of George Washington, who our teacher, also named George, resembled. Mr. Knowlton was one of those rare people who could make anything seem interesting and important, including me.

My self-image took a big leap the day he asked me to read *Robinson Crusoe* and tell the story to the class. I had so much fun that I added to the tale here and there and stretched it out over two days. Mr. Knowlton didn't seem to mind; he got some desk work done. On my report card he wrote: "Bob definitely likes to entertain. I enjoyed his version of R. Crusoe." Mom wasn't sure how to take that but decided that if I had a gift she should nurture it, so I started speech lessons with Leola Merrill— you know, like *My Fair Lady* type lessons: "The...Rain...in...Spain...." Meanwhile, I continued to be the class clown, but I became a much better-read clown.

Playing softball on the school's rock and weed strewn dirt field was about the only recess athletic activity offered to kids at Old Hilltop. After some practice, I developed a fair batting eye and could catch fly balls most of the time, but grounders were another matter. More often than not, the ball would take an odd bounce on our ragged field and blow past or clobber me. Fortunately, the fact that I could hit the ball now and then usually kept me from being chosen last...a dreaded happening.

There's no accounting for DNA; my dad was a good baseball player, sometimes performing in city all-star and Lion's Club donkey baseball games. My father's best friend, Barney, got a lot of laughs at those events by shouting out to donkey-mounted Dad, "Heh Alton, which one's the ass?"

Though the Federal School Lunch program wasn't created until 1946, old Hilltop had its own brand of school lunch that, in retrospect, seemed an awful lot like that served in German prisoner-of-war camps. Bowls of Spanish rice (something of a tomato and oniony nature) and rice and raisins (pretty much as described) were leading menu items, oft repeated. Yuck! Celery stalks, carrots, and small cartons of chocolate milk helped keep me alive.

Valentine's Day was a huge thing in grade school. We'd each drop valentines for every kid in the class into a big heart-decorated box sitting at the front of the classroom. Hand-made valentines were best, especially if they came from a girl you liked. But store-bought ones were okay, particularly from boys, who usually couldn't make very good valentines. But, you had to come up with something...we all kept score.

To understand how an east wind could affect Valentine's day, you have to understand *our* east winds. These started with the appearance of a flat, ominous gray cloud in the canyon sky above the cemetery. When we saw this portent, we knew we were in for it! As wind gusts roared, our windows would sing and threaten to blow out. We didn't have to be told that semi-trucks on the lower road had blown over...that was a given. Anyone who ventured outside could be seen leaning into the wind and walking with caution. As a rule, I could stay home if the wind was accompanied by snow and blizzard conditions, but if it wasn't snowing—"Bundle up, Bob."

One fateful east wind day, Mom packed all of my valentines into a sack and put it in my coat pocket before she kissed me and pushed me out the lee door. I braced against the wind and began the long trek to school. There was some residual snow on the ground, and few minor snowdrifts, but at least it was sunny. Near my destination, I reached a gloved hand into my pocket to see if my valentines were still there, but as I pulled it out, the sack came with it and my valentines escaped. Though I rescued a few, most were last seen tumbling and soaring toward the Great Salt Lake.

I cried my way to school and reluctantly told my sad story. Not to worry. The girls pitched in and helped me make some new valentines to replace those I hadn't captured, and Valentine's Day had a happy ending. Even in high school, the occasional person—usually a girl—would reminisce about my disaster: "Remember that Valentine's Day and the east wind?" *Oh yeah!*

On rare occasions, I'd feign illness to avoid school. My mother had a strict school avoidance policy: I had to have a fever over 101 degrees Fahrenheit. Anything less and I was out the door. I soon learned that I could get the requisite temperature by rubbing the tip of the mercury filled thermometer ever so gently on the bed-sheet or by holding it in front of a warm air vent. If the mercury jumped too high, I could always shake it down a bit. This worked well for a while, but on one occasion Mom surprised me as I was shaking the mercury down from 105 degrees. She caught me at 103. "I don't think so...," she said as she felt my cool brow. So I trudged the mile to Old Hilltop, uphill both ways, as the saying goes.

ATTITUDE ADJUSTMENT

There were only two really good things I can remember about South Davis Junior High School: topping this short list was the cafeteria kitchen. I volunteered to work there because they gave me a large free lunch and the power to decide how big a scoop of mashed potatoes to give my friends. Second on the good thing list was a guy who played a musical saw in a lyceum assembly. For a while, I even saved my money to buy one of those compelling instruments, but where do you find a musical saw teacher?

The major bad thing about the school was a sadistic coach who tried to destroy this gangly kid's already meager self-confidence. In the coach's health class, of all things, he would single out a favorite victim he caught talking, usually me, and make me trudge to the front of the class for "attitude adjustment." After I'd assumed the position, he would gleefully, and sometimes repeatedly, whack my small buttocks with a long paddle that had multiple air holes drilled in it for speed. Years later, when the revered old coach retired, I was asked to contribute toward a present for the elderly mentor. I said that I would if the gift was one of those large bronze fists with the middle finger extended.

Farm work had made me wiry, so I thought I'd give the marching band's sousaphone a try. I loved the way the guys dipped and waved those big horns at football games and in parades. Sadly, those things were heavier than I'd bargained for. At the end of each marching practice I thought my shoulder had been separated from my neck. But I kept at it and gradually became second chair tubist. Unfortunately, I heard "together now tubas...together" quite often. But then came the moment of truth: the first chair failed to show up for a major parade and I became the *only* chair.... I should have taken up the musical saw...or the accordion.

BROWN AND GOLD

Davis was the only high school in Davis County in the early 1950's (The county now has seven large public high schools). My first week there made me feel like I'd escaped from the middle ages. Though a few cliques from the two junior highs persisted, most kids were friendly and were just trying to survive...like me. The teachers seemed to be interested in more than just crowd control, so most classes were bearable and some even fascinating. I sucked in math and had to paddle hard, but I could stay with the flow in most other classes, even excelling in some like anatomy and physiology. But our high school colors—*brown and gold*—get serious. And how do you cheer for a dart (we were the Davis Darts)?

Observing my Dad for years, I had learned a thing or two about being a master of ceremonies, so I became a frequent fixture in school's assemblies. I'd ad-lib and ham it up, which seemed to go over big in our high school. My lame humor, Raymond Pierotti's professional (we thought) Adagio dancing, and some football players wearing dresses formed the nucleus for more than one school production. I gravitated to speech, acting, and play production classes because Iola Merrill's speech lessons had given me a leg up...and there were a *lot* of girls there.

A yo-yo craze prompted my first shop project. I built a one-foot in diameter lathe-turned wooden yo-yo that two friends helped me drop down a two-story stairwell during recess. Though scores of curious and enthusiastic fans lined the banisters cheering, their cheers turned to groans when the heavy disk only made it halfway back up its rope. But the girls loved it: "You'll do better next time," we heard repeatedly. The Wright brothers must have heard similar encouragement early on, and they did all right.

My shop final was a dark green Naugahide-covered desk with matching industrial linoleum desktop and bleached blonde wooden trim and handles (fashionable at the time). Though not a prizewinner, my mom loved it because it matched the fancy decor she had chosen for the oldest student bedroom Dad had built in the vacant coal bin area of the basement. Funny, I'd never seen anything quite like that desk before...nor have I since. I'd once heard that the Smithsonian was interested in obtaining it for its Americana exhibit.

I'm not sure why I dropped into the musty wrestling gym one day, but I made the team at 137 pounds. All that heavy farm work for Gunter had paid off. Being skinny and tall ("The Spider") seemed to be an advantage in most wrestling matches, but not with Brigham City's Nakamura, another farm boy. "The Nak" had short, thick, powerful legs that he locked around my waist like a boa constrictor before he unceremoniously rode me around the wrestling mat like a pony. He resisted my best efforts to unseat him. Either he had no private parts or they were impervious to the pain I tried to inflict on them. That bronc rider went the distance and beat me, not the kind of thing you want to have happen at a home match when your dad is watching and cheerleaders are cheering. But fortunately, there weren't many Nakamuras, and he moved up a weight class before the state meet, which gave me a fighting chance.

As a wrestler, I was always under considerable pressure to make my designated wrestling weight. I would avoid water, sweat, spit, and evacuate everything prior to the afternoon weigh-in. Then I would hurriedly start drinking fluids and ravenously eat, hoping to get some strength back by the time I had to wrestle that evening. Then just before the match—like many other nervous Mormon athletes—I'd sneak into a toilet stall and pray...not that I would win (too presumptuous), but that I would *not* be humiliated. Throughout three years of high school and two years of university wrestling my ritual seemed to work pretty well—except for Nakamura, of course.

Unfortunately, a photo of Nakamura's ride appeared in the *Davis Dart*, our school paper. This provided considerable amusement for my buddies, but it did give me more name recognition, which helped me get elected student body president. Mom's advice, "Bob, always be friendly, to *everyone*," probably helped with that as well. But I think I was blessed with the friendly gene.

A UTAH MAN AM I

In 1951, I became a midshipman wanna-be-warrior at the University of Utah. A NROTC scholarship provided my tuition, books, and a fifty-dollar-a-month stipend (generous for the time). With free room and board at home, I was in fat city. In return, the Navy required that I take some naval science courses, major in some type of engineering, wear my uniform to class once each week, participate in weekend drill sessions every Saturday, and cruise with the Navy or Marines for six weeks each summer. Was that great, or what? But wait, there's more: after graduation, a grateful president planned to award me a regular USN commission, like those given to the graduates of the Naval Academy...my cup runneth over!

The summer cruises opened a new world to me, so I'll mention those first. A small destroyer, the USS Glennon (DD-840), was my first cruise-ship. It tossed me around the North Atlantic for two foul-weather weeks. That tender craft rolled 45 degrees to each side and pitched 25 degrees up and down. I was berthed in the forward end of the ship, separated from the hull-pounding ocean by a quarter inch of steel. I thought about that fact when the sea was rough, which was almost constantly. Positive and negative G-forces toward the bow, coupled with wrenching side to side tilt, could make you sink to the floor, roll off a bunk, fall off a ship's ladder, or float as if in outer space, so you had to get your sea legs early. Surprisingly, I didn't get seasick, but the two bunkmates above me did, so I might as well have. Some midshipmen on the accompanying battleship, the USS Missouri (BB-63), became seasick just watching our destroyer dip and toss about as we came alongside to refuel.

Mercifully, all this was forgotten once we went ashore and saw Paris, then Lisbon, and later Cuba in the time before Castro. Utah Bob's eyes were opened and his life changed forever. As the old WWI song asks: "How ya gonna keep 'em down on the farm (or in Davis County, for that matter) after they've seen Paree?"

The seas settled down on the way to Cuba, so we were exposed to what passed for humor on the Glennon. The forward compartment crew head (toilet) consisted of a long metal trough and seat complex that was welded to the hull on one side. Seawater entered the forward end of the trough and rapidly passed down its length, beneath the seats, before exiting aft. A favorite crew prank was to surreptitiously set fire to a piece of newspaper soaked in lighter fluid and toss it into the trough at the intake end. The fiery missile would swoosh under the rear ends of those seated as it sped to the drain—dramatic to say the least. Old hands would ignore the annoyance, but it certainly got us newbies' attention!

During my stint in the ships engine room spaces, I was amazed at how much could be communicated using many "m---f" expletives, the occasional word, and vigorous finger points. It was a true art form. But I still get nauseated when I think of the bunker fuel smell that saturated those engine rooms, my clothing, and my skin while I was on that rotation.

Each time the destroyer was dockside, its water tanks were filled with fresh water, but after a week or so at sea, water rationing usually became necessary. A burly bosun's mate with a stop watch controlled all shower activity; he allowed each of us ten seconds to wet down...all the time needed to soap up...but only ten seconds to rinse off before he abruptly turned off the water. *"Next!"* One had to prioritize, maybe even wash something different each day.

When off watch, I spent much of my time standing in the ship's bow, overwhelmed by new sensations: breathtakingly beautiful cloud formations and sunsets, squalls, distant waterspouts, flying fish scattered about the fo'c'sle deck in the early morning, and the fresh, clean, salt air. I never tired of watching the bow wake swirling new abstract patterns and wondering how many (if any) other human beings had sailed above the exact same spot on the ocean-floor I was then passing over, sometimes accompanied by dolphins.

The second summer, I split the six-week stint between the Marines at Little Creek, Virginia, and the naval aviators at Brownsville, Texas. The Marines thought they'd recruit me with a mini-boot camp and an amphibious landing. Get serious...I could see where that was heading. And I hadn't forgotten the "Black Shoe" surface Navy's North Atlantic destroyer fiasco the year before...ugh! So when the "Brown Shoe" flyboys promised me clean beds, good meals, regular hours, and all the airplanes I could fly (highlighted by an acrobatic ride in the back seat of a T-33 jet trainer), I said to myself, "Where do I sign up?"

My mind didn't change when they again sent me to Paris via Cherbourg, France, as an upper classman *on* the battleship Missouri...same old stuff but more space. But I did have fun helping navigate the big warship (on which the Japanese signed the WWII surrender document) from France to Guantanamo Bay, Cuba, in the days before satellites or inertial guidance. We had to use dead reckoning and the sun and stars to determine the ship's approximate position. We're talkin' ancient stuff here.

I was put ashore in Norfolk, Virginia, and hitchhiked home via New York City. This adventure was only possible because freeways had not yet replaced the cross-country road system, and hitchhiking in America was not considered as dangerous as it is today. Before air travel became so convenient and inexpensive, businessmen were often driving long distances as part of their jobs, so they were glad to have someone to talk to and help drive. I met interesting people and saw a large chunk of this great country.

But I needed to make big money before school started, so I got a job as a flagman on the new freeway being built through Davis County. I couldn't believe that you could get paid that much money for doing so little. Then, without warning, a huge, spiked sheepsfoot roller dirt compactor backed up to my head and almost compacted me into a waffle. I decided that those big bucks must be like flight pay in the Navy...you never know.

During the school year at the University of Utah, I lived at home and commuted with friends. It soon became apparent that, if I was going to have any social life, I had to become a chick magnet, or associate with guys who were. I joined the Pi Kappa Alpha fraternity in my freshman year and after a long pledge quarter, a miserable goat week, and an initiation overflowing with "...never to be divulged..." secrets, I became a full-fledged brother.

It was disheartening that, even when I became president of the fraternity in my senior year, I couldn't get the members to do away with goat week hazing. "It brings all the brothers closer together," I was told—perhaps the more sadistic ones.

During my goat week, I was briefly excused from the milieu of sleep deprivation, vile food, paddling for minor infractions, and verbal abuse so I could go on a special mission for the goat master: I was ordered to sneak into a sorority house bedroom and crawl in bed with one of the girls. When she screamed, I was to shout, "Oh my God, isn't this the YMCA?" Then I was to jump out the open window and run back to the brothers who would "snatch" me out of there. Nice plan, but the girl didn't scream. Not to worry—after bellowing out my short spiel, this snatchee was out of there anyway, only to find that my nervous snatchers had vanished...valiant brothers. Today's sorority girl would have dropped me with her father's 9mm Glock before I got around to the punch line. If not, the possibility of attempted rape and assault charges, followed by fifteen or twenty years in prison, would have made me pause.

On the positive side, the fraternity did give me a place to hang out between classes, meet a few fine women at social events, and develop some creative skills. I wrote a "Dream Girl" (our fraternity's yearly favorite woman) song that all the brothers sang at the Kingsbury Hall Homecoming competition. We lost that one. But in my junior year, I sang bass in a harmonizing quartet of fraternity brothers that won first place at Homecoming. Our success was in part because we looked splendid in matching powder blue suits that one of our quartet members, a clerk in J. C. Penny's men's clothing department, special ordered and had altered for us to wear for that gig. He collected those suits after the show, undid the alterations, and put them up for sale on Penny's rack the next day.

To impress new rushees (those we hoped to "pledge" as new members), it was thought that the fraternity should have a brother in the University's Skull and Bones and Owl and Key societies, so they told me what school activities counted and I worked to become the guy. The brothers also helped me get elected Associated Men's Students president when I was a senior. It was never clear to me what the exact duties of the AMS officers were when we met four times a year, but we were each given a free white wool cardigan sweater, which sported a big red "U" and an appropriate logo. Except for the logo, that sweater was almost a mirror image of the red letter-sweater with the white "U" they had given me for wrestling. Schools were really into sweaters in those days.

I was fleetingly famous around the Greek community because of my old yellow 1942 Plymouth convertible that had bald tires and a leaky top. It was in great demand for parades and to haul sorority rushees around. But I was no fool—I went with the car. Even in the winter, when the car's top was up, it had so many holes in it that the difference between top up and top down was minimal. Unfortunately, cruising around in Old Yeller was the closest thing to a "chick magnet" experience I could come up with in my undergrad years.

The Navy reminded me that, though military science, wrestling, and the fraternity were all good, I needed to pick out an engineering major. I first tried chemical engineering. The science of chemistry I understood, but my labs left something to be desired. While my friends could get the expected white powder as a yield, mine was usually yellow or beige. My math skill was an additional problem. Though my brothers are great in math, as are my sons, I was always hanging on by my fingernails...not what you'd expect of your average engineer.

By chance, I discovered that I had a talent for mechanical drawing and, as we know, Miss Walsh's first grade deportment closet had helped me develop my artistic right brain, so the Department of Architecture seemed a good fit. To my relief, the Navy agreed.

I found that I had a knack for architectural design, drawing and model making. Though architectural projects required that I spend many late nights, all-nighters, and weekends working in the department and at home, I loved it. I learned almost as much from gifted fellow students as I did from the department's eager and inspirational professors. I graduated with a BFA in architecture and an appreciation for all things beautiful.

"Spring Flowers of the Wasatch" was an affectionate term for a local flora and fauna botany class that contributed to my appreciation of the beauty around me. Energetically led by octogenarian Walter P. Cottam, we explored Salt Lake City and its environs to study the best examples of tree and shrub varieties, sometimes "the only one in town," or "the only one west of the Mississippi." Our elderly mentor, who seemed to know each tree or shrub personally, affectionately introduced us to these friends.

During a field trip into the mountains east of the city, Dr. Cottam told us to meet him at the top of a hill to see a unique conifer, and then he took off up the steep trail at a fast pace. I was wrestling at the time and was in pretty good shape, but I was puffing harder than he was when we reached the top. I sat down on a rock outcropping beside our aged, but still very agile, professor as he shook his head and remarked, "I like to see those folks down there struggling...keeps me young."

After my pre-graduation physical examination for naval air training, I was told that I had some small cavities in my teeth that had to be filled before I could be accepted. Because this had to be done within the week, I was given an appointment with a retired navy dentist who often helped out in urgent situations. Unfortunately, the good doctor could only give me *one* appointment in that time frame.

After examining my teeth and the dental x-rays, the old fellow said that he didn't have time, or think it was safe, to inject Novocain on both sides, upper and lower, but he offered to drill and fill all seven cavities immediately…without analgesia. I agreed, but soon discovered what the inquisition must have been like. This was before they'd developed the air-driven drill, or before he'd seen fit to buy one, so I could feel every electrical-mechanical moment. After he'd drilled the first two or three teeth, I thought that it couldn't get worse—but I was wrong. He kept shouting: "Not long now! Not long now!" If I'd been a prisoner of war experiencing this interrogation technique, I would have told them everything—signed anything! Pale, disheveled, and sweat-stained, I unsteadily shuffled out of his office. He shook my hand as I left and said with a warm smile, "I hope that this is the low point of your naval career, young man."

A CARRIER PILOT, NO LESS

After university graduation in 1955, I became a newly commissioned ensign in the Navy, leaving behind a recently acquired fiancée, Claudia. I reported to NAS (Naval Air Station) Pensacola, Florida, to start a three-and-one-half year adventure. Claudia gave it up after six months and married a lawyer. Now that I had a steady job, my first purchase was a used, bright red 1952 Chevy convertible. Though it had an underpowered Powerglide two-speed automatic transmission, and could barely make it up steep hills, it was sexy, the canvas top didn't leak, and the whitewall tires had tread, a definite step up. Nice wheels for a fledgling pilot.

After ground school, I began flight lessons in the venerable SNJ. This Navy version of the Air Force's AT6 Texan had a stronger airframe, a more powerful radial engine, and the requisite tail hook for carrier landings. This was the Navy's basic flight training workhorse in the post-World War II and Korean War eras. Though a gas-guzzler, it was a reasonably forgiving all-in-one training platform for formation flying, acrobatics, gunnery, dive bombing, and carrier landings. In fact, the SNJ was much more tolerant of student error than some flight instructors. On that subject, I was lucky to have had only one "screamer" (a flight instructor who screams at you for any mistake, and sometimes for no reason at all). I forgave him because a student pilot had almost killed him in a landing incident we'd all heard about.

My first solo flight at a remote, outlying airstrip was uneventful and my landings were pretty good, if I do say so. I'd dropped my instructor off at the landing end of the runway so he could observe my effort, and I was expecting a positive statement or two when he climbed back in the plane. He said nothing until we were in the air, but then casually remarked into the intercom, "Glad you're still alive, Rose...I'd have had a long walk home."

Learning to join up and fly in formation was not easy. The hardest thing for me to learn was to focus *only* on the plane I'd joined up on and not look around to see how everyone else was doing, which could be scary. The barely perceptible adjustments of the throttle and stick required to maintain position weren't as tough to master as I'd thought, but a Blue Angel I was not.

Enough of my color-tagged bullets struck the airplane-towed gunnery target sleeve on check flight to qualify, but I was surprised they had. The tracer bullet path seemed to be all over the place, not straight and steady as you see in old war movies. It's doubtful I would have been an ace in WWII, or WWI for that matter. None of us envied the pilot of the plane that towed that target sleeve: They found three green stained bullet holes in his plane's tail section when he landed (I kid you not). Happily, my bullet markers were red.

Dive-bombing was a blast! It required almost hypnotic concentration to keep the bombsight focused on the target as the plane's fully extended wing flaps caused it to drift. "PULL UP!" yelled an observer as my plane plunged through the designated release altitude on my live-bomb-drop final exam—I was just following that old bomb right in.

Carrier qualification was required of all Navy student pilots before they received advanced training in anything, so the finale of my basic training was to execute six acceptable carrier landings. A new generation of more powerful naval jet aircraft was being introduced into the fleet, as were large "canted deck" aircraft carriers. These huge vessels made it possible for jets to approach at a safe speed, and go around again, if a plane's tail hook failed to catch a wire (stopping cable) or if the plane was waved off (denied permission to land) for any reason. But for the time being we were stuck in the Jurassic period with old dinosaurs like our piston driven, radial engine SNJ, so they taught us carrier-landing techniques essentially unchanged from WWII: straight-ahead approaches and landings on a relatively small aircraft carrier, just like in the old war movies.

At airspeeds barely above a stall, we practiced landing patterns around a small carrier shaped area of paved runway at Bairn Field, near Pensacola. The final approach was barely above treetop level, which made us pucker on occasion. A Landing Signal

Officer (LSO)—standing at the end of the runway with a paddle in each hand—controlled our approaches, as he would on the carrier. At the end of one session, a member of our practice group noticed that there was a small, fresh pine branch caught in one of his plane's wheel assemblies. That made us pucker even more.

The LSO would be replaced by an automated light display ("flying the ball") on the newer carriers. But for now, he still had a job ensuring that we approached the old carrier's flight deck safely, which he'd acknowledge with a cut (throttle back) sign for landing. If the approach appeared unsafe, or if the deck was cluttered, we'd get a wave off. When the thrust power was cut, our aircraft would stall and drop to the carrier deck in a controlled crash. Hopefully, the plane's hook would catch one of three arresting wires in the process and come to a sudden stop. If not, beyond the wires there was a steel cable barrier elevated off the deck. In the rare instance *that* didn't stop the careening plane, it went over the side into the water far below.

On the big day, our formation of four planes circled the Saipan, waiting our turn in the carrier's landing pattern. That proverbial postage stamp down there looked pretty darned small. It didn't add to my confidence that there was a destroyer tailing the carrier...to retrieve crash survivors, if any, from the water. My first approach seemed textbook quality to me. But instead of the cut I'd expected, I got a wave-off. That surprise took me a split second to process before I "applied the coal" (sudden full throttle). Alas, I over-corrected a bit, so the plane tilted up and seemed to be heading toward the carrier's island (superstructure) on the right. But the old yellow workhorse—probably used to this treatment—quickly responded to my jerky adjustment and saved us both. I glanced down at the ship's island as I passed by it. The carrier's skipper (commanding officer) looked up at me and shook his head.

On my second pass, I got a definite cut and pounded in for a landing that almost jerked my head off. The flight deck crew began motioning frantically, but the only signal I recognized was "cut your engine." *Oh crap! This is it! They want me out of the plane.* Then abruptly, my aircraft tilted to the right. In no more than sixty seconds, the left wing lowered and I saw the "start your engine" signal, followed by "apply takeoff power." I'd blown a tire and they'd changed it—that's all. *Whew!* By comparison, my remaining five landings were a cakewalk. There was no mention of my first pass screw-up at debriefing. With so many loose cannons crashing aboard the ship that day, I guess they had bigger fish to fry. *I did it! Can you believe it? I did it!*

After the Korean War, reduced manpower needs in the fleet caused advanced training confusion at NAS Brownsville, Texas, where they sent me next. I first trained in the propeller-driven AD Skyraider, followed by the T33 jet trainer, and the underpowered F9F Panther jet, but at least I was in the jet pipeline, I thought. Then abruptly, I was ordered to fly the propeller-driven twin-engine Beechcraft SNB trainer, so I could spend the next twenty years landing on carriers in the cramped and noisy S2F Tracker twin-engine sub-hunter—get serious.

Then a miracle: a severe, persistent headache, and some cerebrospinal fluid changes (probably viral meningitis), got me out of Brownsville and into the naval hospital at Corpus Christi. While the Navy doctors were trying to determine the nature of my illness—in no apparent hurry—I almost recovered from it. Then, by chance, or divine intervention, a ward nurse pushed my wheelchair and me past the "gedunk" (convenience store) bulletin board, where I saw a notice soliciting volunteers for a new "LTA" starting class at Brunswick, Georgia. "What in the heck is LTA?" I asked my philosophic jet jockey hospital roommate. "Some say it's paradise, Rose—nirvana." *OK then...where do I sign up?*

BOB'S LIGHTER THAN AIR BASE

Pensacola, Florida, the cradle of Naval Aviation, was historic and grand, full of stately live oaks draped with Spanish moss. In contrast, a forest of spindly pines dotted the landscape of my new digs at NAS Glynco, near Brunswick, Georgia. These scrawny evergreens imparted a more blue-collar type of southern charm.

The airfield was midway between Savannah, Georgia, and Jacksonville, Florida, both good for weekend liberty. Nearby were the "Marshes of Glynn," made famous in the post-civil war South by a Sydney Lanier poem. St. Simons Island and Sea Island, Georgia, also good rest and relaxation spots, were separated from mainland Brunswick by some of Sydney's famed marshland and two extensions of St. Simons Sound, all spanned by a four-mile-long causeway. I almost met my demise on that overpass, as I'll later recount.

Dominating the mostly flat vista were two immense—1,058 feet long (three and a half football fields), 297 feet wide and 182 feet high—wood-trussed hangars, built during World War II to comfortably accommodate eight blimps each. The huge structures only housed six of the large fleet airships of my era, and it was a tight fit. The high arched trusses of those hangars were particularly striking. While an architecture student, I had done a research project on the arched trussing system of the Mormon Tabernacle in Salt Lake City, so I appreciated the engineering involved and was amazed at how rapidly the navy had built these complicated Douglas-fir structures during the war. (Both hangars were torn down in the 1970s, but a similar wooden blimp hangar, housing an aircraft museum, can still be seen at Tillamook, Oregon.)

An enormous disc shaped "mat" (paved airship launching and receiving area) extended outward from the working doors of NAS Glynco's two hangars, the centerlines of which were perpendicular to each other. An airship runway merged with the mat far across from the hangars. Also connected to the periphery of the big paved circle were several "pads" (paved mooring circles) where blimps could be temporarily parked, their nose cones secured to large red and white pyramid-shaped, multi-wheeled mobile mooring masts. One or more airships—each riding on a single small wheel—could usually be seen circling into the wind on these pads, like weather vanes, waiting to be towed to the mat for take-off, or across the mat to one of the hangars for tail-first docking.

Single and multi-engine propeller driven-airplanes were parked behind the hangars. All airship pilots were expected to stay qualified in fixed-wing aircraft as well as in blimps.

The massive black-roofed hangars, and the few tethered silver blimps about the mat periphery, created a sci-fi scene in the moonlight, particularly when seen from above. This was amplified when the ponderous concrete doors of the lighted caverns opened to expose more creatures inside. Huge floodlights on the hangar brow eerily illuminated the specters' lumbering escape to the endless mat, and thence to the darkened sky. The scene became even more surreal as the airborne beasts pounced on St Simons Island, only their running lights and the small moonlit NAVY on their side suggesting an origin.

Talk about good fortune: I was the first occupant of a spacious, brand spanking new, BOQ (bachelor officer quarters) room, which had an adjacent bathroom that I shared with a good friend and fellow airship pilot, Gene Dickey. All of us single "gas passers" —helium, of course—were housed in one wing of the new facility and were like family. We ate together in the wardroom, relaxed at the nearby "O-club" (officer's club), and got each other blind dates when necessary—usually a mixed blessing. The base's nightly first-run movies only cost ten cents, so we seldom missed a new flick.

The new BOQ wardroom completed my hog heaven. Stewards served three meals a day—all you could eat—which certainly appealed to this gourmand. Gene Dickey loved to joke about yours truly, mouth full and a bread-roll in one hand, holding up the basket for more rolls. But best of all, the cooks supplied the wardroom kitchen refrigerator with snacks we could access at night. On my first snack trip, I switched on the wardroom light to see a black floor suddenly turn spotless clean, as thousands of cockroaches fled for cover. But as we became old friends, those roaches often spelled out "Hi, Bob" with their bodies before they scampered for cover. This was before I became better schooled on the germ theory of disease, so it never affected my appetite.

Outside the main gate of the airbase was a dimly lit steak house that had a 13-foot grand piano covered in faux leopard skin. Sometimes, in the late afternoon, I would play their piano using the chord and embellishment principles taught to me by the infamous Wally Williams. As I became more proficient, the owner would request that I tickle the ivories through happy hour. My reward was a free steak dinner, occasional tips, and the adulation of any women who had become sufficiently inebriated to think that my cleverly covered mistakes were jazz flourishes.

Before integration, there were only "Whites" and "Coloreds" living in the Deep South. The N-word was generally considered proper for anyone not easily recognizable as Caucasian. Whites and people of color still had everything separate in the late 1950s, including: neighborhoods, schools, churches, restrooms, drinking fountains, bars, restaurants, and transportation. Coloreds were forced to sit in the back of busses and trains.

During a weekend visit to a squadron friend's home in rural Georgia, I was treated to a nearby nighttime full-dress Ku Klux Klan meeting—complete with burning cross—a rehearsal for some future violent outing, I suppose. Even for a Caucasian, this hooded display was pretty scary stuff. But fortunately, in 1964 legal segregation ended and these guys became fringe, even in Dixie.

A little theater group on St. Simons Island helped me periodically escape from the Navy to again become a thespian. *The Caine Mutiny, Three Men on a Horse,* and *On the Waterfront,* were just a few of the plays we performed in outdoor theater-in-the-round fashion at the upscale Cloister Hotel on Sea Island—often to standing ovations (easily entertained).

Our director, Abe Morris, was an old retired Hollywood film director (complete with Clark Gable mustache, beret, cigar, and director's chair). Abe taught us a lot about acting, but his imitations of famous stars like John Wayne or Jimmy Stewart were most memorable. Audiences loved them, and so did we.

Our theatre group's prime mover was Jack Henshaw, a chemical engineer for Hercules Powder (explosives) Company, a wire-rimmed glasses kind of guy, who gestured a lot and always kept things in motion. After each play's final performance, Jack would have a big cast party at his house where he would serve champagne made from potatoes, of all things, to any interested party-goers. By freeze-separating the product, he was able to produce two alcohol concentrations that were virtually indistinguishable by color and taste. He considered the process to be the major achievement of his engineering career, so he was generous with both concoctions, but not forthcoming about which was which. It certainly made for interesting parties.

At one of these soirees, we all sat around an LP record player singing songs from *My Fair Lady*, which had just taken Broadway by storm. I was instantly in love with Julie Andrews and decided I would somehow get to New York City and see her in person. Fortunately, one of our blimps was due for repairs at Lakehurst, New Jersey, so I volunteered to help pilot it there (cheapest airfare I could find). I hopped a base bus into the Big Apple for the evening performance (both Julie and Rex Harrison were in it), and loved every minute of it. I stayed that night in a recommended cheap hotel and bummed a flight back to NAS Glynco the next day with an in-transit AD

Skyraider pilot. We compared war stories while we were flying to Georgia. His yarns were much better than mine because he'd actually been in a war.

I definitely needed a sexier mode of transportation than my underpowered red Chevy convertible, so for $1,900 I bought my first new car, a bright red 1957 MGA, which I actually drove off the dock in Jacksonville, Florida. I spent the afternoon helping the guys from the car agency clean the Cosmoline off my little red bomb before I headed back to Brunswick, cautiously avoiding the well-known small-town Georgia radar speed traps. Redneck cops longed to ticket cars like mine. My new auto was cold in winter, hot in summer, and sometimes wet when it rained, but it looked like a chick magnet's car...and it was *mine*!

Hurrying home from St. Simons Island via the four-mile-long Torras Causeway, I almost bought the farm in that little red speedster. Late at night, it was not unusual for young guys like me to use the two-lane (now four-lane) overpass roadway for speed trials, since law enforcement radar couldn't get a reliable reading on the curved and mildly arched span. Acting on a poor-judgment impulse, I decided to see if the car could really do 106 MPH as the speedometer suggested. As I was about to prove that it could, two tiny bright lights suddenly appeared up ahead— *Racooooon!*

I swerved to avoid the animal and came within a few inches of climbing the sidewalk, crashing through the railing, and going over the side. Fortunately, my little sports car's low center of gravity helped save me and I got my careening auto under control. I stopped at mid-span, heart racing, and looked over the side—that black water was a *long* way down! This was before seat belts of any kind, and way before air bags. Another of my nine lives used up, and I wasn't even flying, technically.

Two months later, a guy I knew from the other airship squadron decided to do his own speed trial on the causeway, ironically in a little black MGA that he'd bought after he'd seen mine. He was killed when his car smashed through the side rails and dropped into the water below. I always wondered if my raccoon had done an encore.

ABOUT BLIMPS (A FEW FACTS AND AIRSHIP PRINCIPLES)

I flew blimps, *not* dirigibles. So what's the difference between a dirigible and a blimp? One's rigid and the other's non-rigid. I'll expand on that, include a little history, and add a few basics that should help you appreciate my stories. There'll be a quiz at the end.

The rigid airship, or dirigible (zeppelin in Germany), was a giant cigar-shaped aircraft (The *Hindenberg* was 300 yards long and 7,000,000 cubic feet in volume) that used a rigid skeleton of magnesium and aluminum to maintain its form. Large cylindrical sacks, filled with either lighter-than-air hydrogen or helium gas, produced the lift to keep the ship airborne, helium generating slightly less lift than hydrogen. Multiple airplane engines powered the propeller-driven airship, and large tail fins provided directional control when the dirigible was moving.

During WWI, Germany had used the dirigible for observation and crude bombing, and Great Britain for submarine patrol. But the heyday of rigid airship development was in the mid to late 1930s, just before WWII, when the United States was testing military dirigibles and Germany was successfully flying commercial ones. The last U.S. Navy dirigibles (*Akron* and *Macon*) could hangar five small bi-winged fighter-type airplanes that could be lowered, launched, and recovered by trapeze-like structures protruding from the airship's underside.

The United States' dirigibles were filled with nonflammable helium that we produced but wouldn't export. Germany had no helium supply of its own, so its dirigibles were filled with highly flammable hydrogen. WWI experience with German zeppelins, and the rise of the Third Reich in the 1930's, precluded our changing the helium policy, even for the doomed passenger-carrying *Hindenberg* or the slightly smaller *Graf Zeppelin,* the most successful passenger airship of all time. In nine years, the *Graf* flew over 1,050,000 miles, crossed the Atlantic 144 times, and safely carried more than 13,000 passengers.

Weather was the dirigible's main enemy. It was hard for these gigantic, slowly moving aircraft to fly around weather fronts, and they were extremely vulnerable when attached to a vertical mast on the ground. Weather related crashes were largely responsible for the termination of the American military's rigid airship program in the mid 1930s. The dramatically documented fiery crash of Germany's hydrogen containing *Hindenberg* (Lakehurst, New Jersey on May 6th 1937) ended all commercial ventures as well.

The non-rigid military airship, or blimp, was used rather successfully for antisubmarine warfare and surface ship convoy protection during WWII. The largest operational fleet airship at the time I was flying (1956-58) was over 100 yards long and approximately 1,000,000 cubic feet in volume, much smaller than the dirigible, but five times larger than the Goodyear media blimps of today.

Blimps had no internal skeleton. The one-eighth inch thick envelope (rubber and fabric bag) was cut and fused to a predetermined shape by the Goodyear Tire Company in Akron, Ohio. Then, like a party balloon, it was inflated with helium gas, just enough to keep the bag's shape firm. An alleged benefit of this low internal pressure was that helium would be lost at a slow rate if a bullet or cannon shell hit the blimp. Glad I never had to test this assumption.

Military blimps needed to be a few thousand pounds heavy on takeoff or landing. This was weight not offset by the helium's static (not moving) lift. The airfoil effect of the blimp's shape as it moved through the air—similar to that of an airplane wing—provided the additional dynamic (forward-moving) lift needed to get the ungainly craft off the ground and keep it in the air. In fact, the airship was flown much like an airplane in many respects. It needed powerful engines to provide enough speed to gain elevator (up or down) and rudder (side-to-side) control by its large tail surfaces.

Two large inflatable air cells called ballonets (pronounced: "bal-oh-nays") were fused to the inside floor of the bag, one forward and one aft. Synchronous air inflation of one ballonet, and deflation of the other, caused the helium mass to shift slightly forward or aft to change the aircraft's center of static lift (opposite of center of gravity). This would raise or lower the blimp's nose to help with trim when the blimp was moving. Manipulation of the amount of air in the ballonets also helped keep the pressure inside the whole envelope constant as outside temperatures and pressures changed.

By the time a blimp was ready for landing it would have lost the weight of burned fuel, and perhaps its weapons, and would probably have become too light to land safely. To assess its condition, the crew would "weigh-off" the blimp (stop it in midair and note the rate at which it dropped in altitude if heavy, or ascended if light). To add weight for landing, the ship was slowed down over a body of water and a large bag on a cable was lowered and filled with water. After it was winched back up, the liquid could be pumped into the blimp's ballast tanks. The procedure was repeated until the aircraft was heavy enough for landing.

If one or both engines failed on takeoff, the airship could get airborne by dumping ballast water and gasoline (both held in quick-release tanks), depth charges, and homing torpedoes to lighten ship. In the event of a total engine failure, the whole blimp became a large "free balloon," somewhat like a hot air balloon but silent. Even helium could be judiciously released to maintain a desired altitude until the blimp could be safely crash-landed.

A fact for aircraft enthusiasts: if a moving airship became light for any reason, the pilot's elevator controls reversed (yoke forward to climb—back to descend) as the dynamic lift force was shifted to the underside of the envelope airfoil to create a downward pull, or drag. The blimp would then fly slightly nose down, like an upside-down airplane wing, to keep from gaining altitude. I've been told that the small Goodyear media blimps seen at sporting events are purposely landed light. Sandbags are then attached to keep the ship on the ground until refueling weight can be added.

Takeoff was quite a show. The military blimp's nose was detached from its mobile mast, which was then towed out of the way. Men or powerful "Mules" (four-wheeled winch-machines) pulled on lines attached to the airship's nose, to steady it until takeoff roll had begun and the big tail surfaces could get directional control.

On landing, reverse propeller thrust slowed the blimp to a stop. Then, a combination of men and machines would again steady the nose lines until the mobile mast could be wheeled into position and the blimp's nose-cone-fitting secured. After that, the landing crew could relax…somewhat…as the blimp was towed toward a parking pad or the hangar.

The airship was always vulnerable to the vagaries of weather. You could only feel reasonably comfortable about a blimp when it was in the hangar, though docking into and undocking from the hangar could also be nail-biters, particularly if the wind picked up or changed direction during the operation. If that wasn't enough, even when the blimp was inside the hangar there had to be an inflation watch: two guys, hopefully keeping each other awake, making sure that the bag maintained its internal pressure as the hangar's temperature and pressure changed—are you still awake?

The old movie *The Hindenberg* is worth watching. Two books laden with pictures of rigid and non-rigid airships are also worth looking at: *The Giant Airships*[20] and *Sky Ships*[21].

[20] Botting, Douglas, ed., *The Giant Airships*, Time Life Books, 1981.
[21] Althoff, William F., *Sky Ships: A History of the Airship in the United States Navy*, Orion Books, 1990.

BOB'S BLIMP STORIES

The two primary fleet airships were the large, quadruple-tail-fin, ZPG-2W, radar early warning blimp and the slightly smaller triple-fin ZS2G-1 antisubmarine warfare blimp.

The ZPG-2W airship flew out of Lakehurst, New Jersey, carrying two flight crews totaling twenty men. The off-duty crew slept in a compartment built into the helium containing bag just above the electronic workspace. The ship had a complete galley so that three meals a day could be prepared for the crew. The blimp's mission was to provide fill-in radar coverage in the far north while the "DEW Line" (Distant Early

Warning line) of permanent ground radar stations was being built. The ZPG-2W would usually be out on station above that cold arctic northland for three days at a time. Thank God I wasn't in that outfit.

I piloted a gentleman's airship, the ZS2G-1, which usually flew out on antisubmarine patrols of less than 24 hours. It carried a crew of ten, including four pilots. There was no separate sleeping space, but there were two bunks where crewmembers might catch a nap; they rarely did however because the pounding engines were just outside the crew car on bunk level—undoubtedly planned that way. We had a limited galley but the crew chief could whip up pretty good meals, including a mandatory steak for dinner.

Our blimp had standard submarine detection gear, but we also had a secret weapon: a towed sonar "fish." This nifty, streamlined, missile-shaped hunk could be attached to a cable, winched down to the water, and towed submerged while it searched for a submarine. It was pretty cool when working properly, which was off and on, but even if it wasn't functioning, the sonar's constant pinging had to worry the Russian submariners a bit. In the bomb bay, we carried one or two depth charges and sometimes a homing torpedo. We were a combat-ready weapons system.

The primary mission of Airshipron Two (ZP-2) was to patrol the waters off our lower east coast to detect and pursue Russian submarines. When there was no enemy sub to harass, which was most of the time, the powers that be might surreptitiously send in a U.S. Navy sub to test our capabilities. We almost dropped a homing torpedo on one of these friendly probes that showed up in restricted waters we were patrolling. As luck would have it, just as the submerged target was detected—where none of our subs should be—the blimp's radio receiving capabilities went down, though it could still transmit. Walt Johnson, "Old Tremulous" to those that knew him, kept his quivering hand on the bomb-bay door handle as the blimp, its towed sonar working for once, continuously and elegantly painted the sub with sound. Walt was heard loudly begging seemingly unhearing ears for permission to drop—"at least *something!*"

Another key mission was to keep Russian subs well submerged during satellite launches at Cape Canaveral. This was to keep them from intercepting, jamming, or otherwise interfering with launch telemetry data. Even if the towed sonar wasn't collecting or processing information, we were told to drop the fish in the water, tow it around, and ping up a storm. I guess we introduced some valuable uncertainty or they wouldn't have kept sending us back.

On one such malfunctioning fish-down occasion in deep water off the Florida coast, a Soviet submarine was known to be in our general search area, so we were towing our malfunctioning sonar around—doing our impotent pinging thing. Suddenly, the fish hit something solid and metallic, broke loose, and disappeared. We were all pretty sure that it had collided with the submarine, so everyone hoped that Moscow would be impressed with our fearsome capabilities.

Returning from another of these harassment fiascos, we were scheduled to land at 0800 when there would be plenty of personnel to help with the landing. As we approached NAS Glynco from the south, we encountered a strong gusty north wind, which reduced our groundspeed to near zero. Though we were only fifteen miles from the base, and could easily see the hangars, calculations suggested that it would be quicker, and safer, to land at NAS Guantanamo Bay, Cuba, 900 miles south. Gitmo already had several mobile airship masts and other equipment airship squadrons needed for yearly practice deployments with the fleet. But a trained landing crew nucleus would have to be rapidly flown to Cuba by airplane as soon as the decision to land there was made. Though we were all cheering for the wind, the uncooperative gale eventually decreased enough to allow a normal landing in Georgia.

While on patrol, we often flew over the Gulf Stream. Because of our low cruising altitude of 500 feet, we often saw a rich potpourri of marine animals: large schools of humpback whales, hammerhead sharks, sea turtles, and giant jellyfish, to name but a few. On a slow day, we might circle around and fly lower to investigate. But the most impressive aquatic show I've ever seen was our one-time sighting of a huge school of gigantic manta rays. Extending from horizon to horizon was a carpet of wing-like movements, undulating waves, as if the creatures would become airborne at any second.

Responding to this extremely rare and breathtaking scene, our loose cannon airship commander, "Dauntless Dave" Cummins, proposed dropping a depth charge in their midst—"to see 'em flyyyy!" We talked him out of it, but you can see that ecological sensitivity was about as far along as civil rights at that time.

Training flights over land were a blast. Our five-hundred-foot cruising altitude, combined with the blimp's slow airspeed, gave us an extraordinary view of life below. People would stop what they were doing, call others to come look, wave, and take our picture. If we weren't in a hurry, which we usually weren't, the sight of scantily clad girls waving would make us circle back at a lower altitude so we could wave back at them and show off. Part of the forward lookout's job was to keep an eye out for pretty young women.

Cynthia, a summer girlfriend, went to an all-girl college in Milledgeville, Georgia. As she left to go back to school, she joked, "Drop me a present sometime...you know, if you're flying over." Well, was that a challenge or what? A month later, in the dark, we essentially stopped our airship in midair three or four hundred feet above the campus tennis courts. Down went our water bag, with several teddy bears attached, into the midst of a gaggle of excited college girls blinking their flashlights. When we winched up the bag, we discovered that a big package of cookies had replaced the bears, much to the delight of our crew. As we departed, we noticed that many of the townsfolk were outside blinking their flashlights and spotlights, so we gave them a short burst of our million-candlepower sub-hunting searchlight—a real crowd pleaser, as it turned out. The local newspaper reported that our blimp was: "…like an alien spaceship with a death ray…" and "…as big as our whole town."

I was an instant celebrity on Cynthia's campus and in the community. Two weeks later, the owner of the Bide-A-Wee motel saw me in my dress whites, with navy wings attached, as I was leaving his establishment to accompany Cynthia to a formal dance at the college. When he found out that I had flown "that humongous dirigible" (I didn't correct him) he said, "My man—your room is free!" He introduced me to Earl, a Georgia State Patrolman, who was drinking coffee in the lobby. Trooper Earl wondered if I had seen him flashing his spotlight at me. I said that I had and that's why I'd turned on my big searchlight. He told me that if I ever had trouble with the highway patrol, anywhere in Georgia, I should give him a call and he'd handle it. Fortunately, I never had to test old Earl on that one.

Yes, the public loved us. Except for the Blue Angels, we were the most sought-after flyover in the close-by Southern United States. In fact, on two occasions we were invited to be part of the same air show as the Blue Angels. We could stop our huge aircraft in midair in front of a grandstand and wave to the crowd. They couldn't do that.

One never knew when those endless hours of training flight boredom might be spiced up by a short burst of unanticipated fun. On a moonlit night training flight up the Carolina coast, our ZS2G-1 airship was passing the beach of some billionaire's private island when the forward lookout suddenly reported that the sandy shore appeared to be littered with recumbent nudes. "BATTLE STATIONS!" We continued north for a few miles and then surreptitiously, running lights off, circled inland, eventually heading east for an outbound run toward the coastline at an altitude of less than 200 feet. If our calculations were correct, we would pass over the ocean beach right on target.

A low hill hid our approach and an onshore wind helped mask our engine noise. Just as we popped over the knoll, we flipped on the big searchlight, which lit up the beach below as if it were daytime. Golly me—*what a sight*! Some partygoers tried to run, covering up as best they could, but most didn't bother. Our crew took photographs of the scene below, because there had to be evidence if we were to be believed. At the water's edge, we turned off the searchlight and the darkened airship headed out to sea. All trace of us was gone by the time the revelers got their night vision back. There was considerable jollity at Airshipron Two when the enlarged photos were pinned on the squadron bulletin board, but we all envied those guys on the beach.

For two weeks each winter, half of the squadron (the lucky ones) worked and played in tropical pre-Castro Cuba, while two airships were deployed to NAS Guantanamo Bay to participate in fleet antisubmarine exercises. Before we flew the airships home, clever crew chiefs would steam clean selected water ballast tanks and fill them with dollar per gallon Cuban rum. Once back in Georgia, two or three bottles of bourbon on the back floorboards of the customs officer's car ensured that our water tanks would not be inspected before ecstatic squadron members could off-load and distribute their treasure.

Returning from one Cuba deployment, I was piloting an airship that had two water ballast tanks filled with contraband rum. On takeoff, we encountered an ocean downdraft at the end of the runway, so the command pilot put his hand on the blimp's water valve handles, preparing to dump water to make the blimp lighter. The sound of the roaring engines drowned out the crew's fervent prayers as the big craft slowly settled toward the water. But then, like a wounded bomber in an old WWII movie, the blimp began to slowly gain altitude—prayers answered. Truth be known, we'd have dumped gas before valving the precious cargo in those two tanks.

If routine checks showed an unexplained slow leak of a blimp's helium, we'd put the ship in the hanger so that several daring men, suspended by lines from the roof trusses, could inspect every inch of the bag surface. Invariably, several small round puncture holes would be found. We suspected that the majority of these bullet-holes were due to moonshiners who thought we were the feds—technically correct, I guess—but we were never sure who shot at us. Though the possibility of taking a bullet was always in the back of our minds while flying, to my knowledge, no one was ever killed or wounded by a peacetime gunshot.

We were trained to react to the failure of one or both blimp engines, but I only once saw both machines fail completely, just as an airship was taking off. An airplane would have crash-landed, possibly killing all on board. But the blimp's crew dumped water and fuel to become a free balloon and the craft slowly drifted with the prevailing wind, up and out toward the Atlantic Ocean. We all ran after it, hoping that we could help, but it soon floated over the pine-lined airfield perimeter, and the pilot, Pete Fowler, shrugged his shoulders and waved goodbye.

The crew kept the blimp airborne until it floated over the coastal marshland, where helium was valved and the aircraft gently crash-landed. A large "zipper" on the top of the bag was then ripped open to deflate the envelope, which almost instantaneously settled over the airship's crew-containing car. Using hunting knives they had strapped to their ankles, the crew rapidly (there were poisonous snakes in that marsh) cut their way out through at least two layers of rubber blimp skin. Search planes certainly had no trouble finding that massive silver wreckage, ten guys standing on it, all waving to catch attention.

Fortunately, no airship crewmembers were killed during my tour in ZP-2, but there were three blimp crashes with several fatalities that happened after I left the service, the worst being an experimental ZPG-3W airship disaster at Lakehurst in 1960, a big nail in the future LTA coffin. But airship crashes didn't worry me; I was young, blimps were safer than carrier-based time bombs of my era, and they gave us flight pay!

THE MARK 90—A NUCLEAR OPTION

My final blimp story deserves its own heading (and a little dramatization) because the topic came up at a dinner party many years after it happened and a cautioning squadron mate whispered to me, *"Shhh, Bob! That's still classified."* Anne was there. She's my witness.

In the early 1950's, weapons analysts were squeezing nuclear bombs into every conceivable delivery system. But they had to dig deep into the fantasy pocket to come up the idea of a blimp-delivered nuclear depth charge. To test the proposal's feasibility, and to be sure the weapon wasn't a kamikaze variant, I guess, the "Mark 90 Operation" was devised. One of ZP-2's (Airshipron Two), airships was designated to be the test delivery vehicle.

In the two months preceding this historic flight, an all-volunteer blimp crew trained for the mission in a decked-out new ZS2G-1 airship commanded by Commander Mack Horst, our squadron executive officer. CDR Horst was thought by many to be the best blimp pilot in the navy, having flown antisubmarine airships at the end of WWII and test-landed a blimp on an aircraft carrier. His orders read, "...to train in utmost secrecy...," a strange condition for an aircraft that required a throng of line handlers to help it get airborne and to catch it when it landed. But the ground and airship crews of this soon-to-be-feared menace rapidly became a well-oiled machine, ready for any eventuality, except the one that occurred. Even CDR Horst, who thought he'd seen everything, hadn't.

On the big day, base security was increased and the designated airship was moved to a closely guarded mooring circle adjacent to the huge airship operating mat. Two Navy cargo planes landed on the nearby jet runway, taxied up to the CIC (Combat Information Center), and dropped their rear cargo doors. Out poured jeeps filled with armed guards who were deposited around both planes, at street intersections, and at the active airship staging circle.

A truck with a black, tarpaulin-cloaked mass and several armed guards on its flatbed emerged from one plane's cargo bay. This was NAS Glynco's most exciting day ever. Gawkers from the admin building, commissary, laundry, day care, and the like, quickly lined the road "to see the atom bomb go by." Naval air station scuttlebutt never ceased to amaze me.

The Mark 90 was a cumbersome thing. When it was hung on the blimp's depth charge rack, there was barely enough room to close the bomb bay doors. Apparently, an airship application didn't require finesse.

After this very special depth charge was successfully loaded, our squadron's rotund commanding officer, CDR Keen, climbed aboard the airship to give one last word of encouragement to the crew. Before he'd relinquished command of the ship to

CDR Horst, he'd considered the fact that this historic flight would look good in his promotion folder, but the job would require many long over-water training flights, which he detested. The CO didn't mind the all-night over-land ones so much, because he could entertain himself with the forward lookout's sub-hunting binoculars. One never knew what well-lighted window surprises might be seen from an airship creeping through the darkness, a few hundred feet above the ground.

"... *You're cleared to assume takeoff position,*" crackled a voice from the control tower, the signal for a big tractor to begin pulling the large multi-wheeled pyramidal mooring mast, with blimp attached, off the mooring circle and into takeoff position, far across the mat from the hangars. A silver airship in motion is a beautiful sight, even one carrying a weapon of mass destruction. But things weren't so pretty inside the craft; the CO had just surprisingly announced, "CDR Horst, you're relieved—I'm assuming command!" The crew furtively glanced toward the exits but no one mutinied. *"Cleared for takeoff and good luck,"* said the tower

The engines roared in neutral as Airshipron Two's ground handling personnel steadied the long lines hanging down from the blimp's nose while it was being freed from the mobile mast attachment. Then the red and white pyramidal mast was pulled out of the way. Perching on its one small wheel, the blimp began gradual forward motion into the wind, as the self-appointed airship commander applied thrust to the engines…too slowly, many thought. The line handlers had barely released the nose lines when the wind freakishly shifted and gusted, causing the unusually heavy airship to drift ponderously toward Hangar Two, all the while struggling to gain enough airspeed to become airborne.

The skipper could have quickly dumped water, and even gasoline, to lighten the ship, but he was hesitant and indecisive. Finally, with Hangar Two ever so much closer, he made his only good decision: "IT'S ALL YOURS, MACK!" he shouted as he ran to the back of the airship car and jumped out onto the tarmac (seriously). Though the blimp's wheel was just leaving the ground, the ship's tail down position saved our brave captain from serious injury.

CDR Horst immediately dumped water and fuel, but the large airship still lumbered slowly into the air, gradually pointing away from hanger two, but still drifting down that hangar's upwind side. The blimp clawed for groundspeed and altitude in the now brisk wind, like an old square-rigged sailing ship off a lee shore. Would the blimp's large tail clear the hangar's rear pylon…? Suddenly, the bomb bay doors opened and a large black mass was seen hurtling down toward the back end of the hanger. Everyone tensed—there was no time to duck and cover!

The large, pricey chunk of disposable ballast missed the hangar, but crashed through the wing of a parked SNJ before loudly gouging a small crater in the underlying asphalt. The lightened blimp leapt into the air, like a Red Robin balloon escaping from a child's hand. The tail section missed the hangar's rear pylon by inches.

The excitement now over, the disgraced blimp could be seen slinking out to the Inland Waterway to winch up and pump-aboard seawater for landing ballast. Within thirty minutes, the local radio station was reporting that "an unexploded atom bomb" had been dropped behind the hangar closest to the road. It was stressed that the area should be avoided until the weapon could be safely removed. Lemming-like, a few hundred locals swarmed in, cramming against the fence to get a better look at ground zero, less than two hundred yards away. In a festive mood, some even brought lunches and beer.

One of the trickiest parts of the whole operation was the retrieval of the Mark 90 from the hole it had dug for itself. Men in special suits converged on the site with a wide array of equipment. It was reported to the press that the depth charge was "damaged but not compromised." Materializing out of nowhere, a large crane hoisted the weapon out of its crater and lowered it onto its flatbed truck. The vehicle's driver looked none too happy about his assignment. The truck's grim-faced guards now followed in a jeep…at a discrete distance.

Once the circus was aboard the two cargo planes, their large rear doors were slowly closed and both aircraft took off, heading north…never to be seen again. Airshipron Two's days in the nuclear sun were over.

Though there was no nuclear explosion or radiation leak, there was considerable fallout for CDR Keen. He maintained that he'd jettisoned his 230 pounds to help lighten the ship, but an incident review board was not amused. Our impulsive commanding officer was ordered to Washington DC and, for all practical purposes, disappeared. A visiting air force major seemed to remember hearing about a naval officer named Keen when he was at the Thule Air Base in Greenland—something about blimps and the Dew line—but the fellow was always somewhere in the Arctic when the major flew in.

The blimp version of the Mark 90 never surfaced again. The squadron routine settled back to normal, as did the local paper's letters to the editor. The blessings of cable news frenzy were still far down the pike, so the Navy dodged a large bullet. As the last military airship was deflated in 1962 and crated off to mothballs in Akron, Ohio, it's likely that this secret is safe, particularly when those of us who still remember the story are gone…hopefully of natural causes.

LTA'S CONCLUSION

In 1957 the Navy began decommissioning its airship squadrons on the East Coast, replacing them with fixed wing aircraft and helicopters. The first casualty was NAS Weeksville, North Carolina. Returning from Lakehurst, New Jersey, I was piloting the last airship to land and take-off at Weeksville before it was closed. (That same ZS2G-1 blimp, possibly with me aboard, is depicted on page 236 of the *Sky Ships* reference.)

As we were preparing to leave Weeksville and fly home, a supply chief in a pickup truck sped up to our boarding ladder, handed up a large box, and pled with our crew chief, "Please get this damn thing out of here. It's not on any inventory list, and we don't want to be caught with it." I became busy with the take-off and thought no more about it. But the next day I returned to my BOQ room to find a new pair of large sub-hunting binoculars on my bed. "Navy Surplus" was scrawled in large script on an attached tag.

In 1962, the lighter-than-air program ended. A fitting final tribute to LTA is a quote from page 264 of *Sky Ships*: "Today at Lakehurst station only the brooding hangars recall four decades of lighter-than-air-aeronautics. But this place remains synonymous with Navy LTA. The thoughtful visitor can reflect on the experiment that was focused here. One can cross the hangar deck where the *Shenandoah* was built and the *Los Angeles* was dismantled. The landing field is just outside where the *Acron* lifted off for the last time—and where the wreckage of *Hindenburg* fell. Across the empty mat are the twin hangars built for the urgent days of World War II. From these the K-ships departed on wartime patrol. The old mooring circles for the big ships (rigids) are long gone, but several for the postwar blimps remain, crumbling and forgotten among the scrub. Younger visitors don't notice them. But an older generation remembers. The U.S. Navy's lighter-than-air machines are history. The men who flew them have long since retired. But these aircraft and aviators helped to advance the science of aeronautics. They should not be forgotten."

That's why I've included these stories. I was fortunate to have been part of the final act—it was great fun!

ROBERT WAY/LISA

In 1958, just before I was discharged from the Navy, I met Francis Agnes Highsmith, a Southern belle from St. Simons Island, Georgia. Her father, E. Way Highsmith, a retired lawyer, owned the "10, 2 and 4 Ranch," a plantation property that abutted the Marshes of Glynn. The ranch had been formerly owned by the inventor of the world's first major carbonated commercial soft drink, Dr. Pepper. A 1950s company slogan begged folks to drink their product at each of the three daytime hours ("Dr. Pepper Time") mentioned in the ranch's name. Fran and I were married just before I exited the service and we soon returned to Utah so that I could concentrate on getting into medical school. Robert Way Rose (Wayde), born in the summer of 1959, was the first of my handsome and intelligent children (and grandchildren), and the apple of my eye.

As we labored through medical school, it became apparent to Fran and me that we had little in common, except Wayde, so we were divorced in the latter part of 1963. Fran and Wayde moved to Seattle soon after I entered pediatric practice in Bellingham, so he was able to visit us some weekends and in the summer. The memory of his little face peering out of the bus window each time he left Bellingham for Seattle still haunts me.

But to lighten things up, I'd like to tell a few short anecdotes about Wayde at various ages, even though they might be out of chronologic sequence with the rest of my narrative.

Wayde gave Anne a goldfish for a Christmas present, so she asked him to name it—"Tootsie Anvil" was like another child to us until Matt was born. When we traveled, Tootsie went too, in a thermos. After Matt's birth, less attention was paid to Tootsie, so she started jumping out of her fish bowl, because of jealousy we thought, but how did we know? Alas, poor Toots made one unobserved jump too many. When Wayde next visited, he wanted to see where Tootsie was buried. Fortunately, I had seen this one coming and had put up a little grave marker.

Showing considerable creativity, Wayde directed and produced war videos with his Seattle neighborhood friend's and spent many hours in Bellingham drawing long comic strips on calculator paper. He invented "The Island Olympics," a sailing vacation game that the boys played when we rowed ashore to the various San Juan Islands. His brothers were rewarded with large aluminum foil medals, which made the competition fierce. But Wayde's most remembered creation was a Christmas nativity play that starred his brothers, cousins, and Skippy, our black Dachshund, who masqueraded as a white sheep with shaving cream wool...until the wool melted.

Wayde loved model railroads and had a room full of them. Because of his hobby, one Saturday we all piled in the car and drove to Seattle so we could take in the Western States Model Railroad Show at the Olympic Hotel. As we got closer to downtown Seattle, traffic slowed to a snail's pace. Wayde was beside himself: "Dad, we should have left earlier; these cars are beating us out.... With so many cars lining up we'll never find a parking place anywhere near the hotel.... If we do find a parking place, we'll never get in!" But as we reached Seattle's North 45th Street exit, the long line of cars peeled off and headed to Husky Stadium for the football game and we had smooth sailing to the hotel. We parked easily and, because Saturday morning attendance was light, we saw all of the displays at our leisure. But this family experience gift keeps on giving; when two or more of us are in an auto behind a long line of cars in slowed traffic, anywhere, someone is almost certain to say, "There must be a model railroad show."

I'm *now* told that Wayde's fascination with trains led to his searching for unlocked Burlington Northern train track switches he could throw. "Dad, I always turned them back!" With his little brother Matt tagging along, he also placed pennies on the tracks so they could watch the train wheels flatten them. Now *that* I can live with.

Wayde loved sailing, so Anne and I learned to sail. We raced and cruised our keelboat, *Skye*, (discussed later) for four years and then downsized to a trailerable "420" racing dingy that we could sail on Lake Chelan and Silver Lake. Then came our last downsize, to windsurfers. Aboard one of these, Wayde tried to cross Hale's pass from Lane Spit to the Lummi Indian reservation. The incoming current was running at nearly six knots, in excess of our windsurfer's top speed of four. Over the next hour, Wayde's course made good (Navy term) was not east toward the reservation but north toward far distant Sandy Point.

His brothers and I borrowed a friend's Boston Whaler and rushed to the rescue, but as we came alongside, an exhausted and bedraggled Wayde shouted, "KEEP ON GOING! KEEP ON GOING! I DON'T WANT TO BE EMBARASSED!"

Matt and Wayde enjoyed each other's humor. Their Canadian accented "You ever been to Port Alberny...eh?" was accepted as genuine on the ski slopes. They could both break up laughing about the Lakeway Apartment's "Merry Xmas" sign and Anne's home-bottled root beer that they were sure contained at least two percent alcohol, a suspicion they never mentioned to her for fear she'd quit making it. As our car once passed an "Entering Happy Valley" sign, Wayde said, "Oh, I suddenly feel *so* happy, don't you, Matt?" Matt agreed and they milked it for a while. Needless to say, as we passed the "Leaving Happy Valley" sign we had to hear that shtick as well.

Wayde did very well in high school, graduating as valedictorian with a 4.0 GPA. He won a full scholarship to Stanford University, where he graduated with a 3.8 average in mechanical engineering. Once, after he had completed a product design class, the professor smiled at him for the first time and said, "You have the ability to think of things that are truly useful...don't ever lose that."

Early robotics development at Westinghouse didn't do it for Wayde, so he gained acceptance to the prestigious film school at USC, where he found filmmaking fun but not a good fit. He became a computer consultant in Los Angeles, California, while he was apparently struggling with other issues that I would have never have suspected were present.

Wayde changed the playing field completely, in 1988, by taking the necessary steps to become "Lisa." The effect of this action on all of our lives was enormous. At first, Anne and I were deeply saddened by this radical change in Lisa's life. It was hard to understand and there was little information available then. But with time, we've gotten to know and love Lisa as the daughter we'd never had. Brad soon came to grips with this passage but it took Matt longer because of his closeness to Wayde. Matt and Lisa began getting to know each other again in 2006 and we've had some great family Christmas (Xmas) parties with Lisa since.

After several months of abdominal pain, and some weight loss, Lisa was diagnosed with Non-Hodgkin Lymphoma and underwent extensive chemotherapy. At present, she is at least in remission and hopefully cured.

Though Lisa received a master's degree in psychology from California State University in Los Angeles, she chose to return to the technology field and is presently employed at a subsidiary of Apple Computer Co. She is very good at software development and testing, so the Apple Corporation has repeatedly shown their appreciation with bonuses and advancements. Lisa lives by herself in Mountain View, CA, near Palo Alto, where she recently bought her first non-condo house and has been remodeling it. She has an active social life that includes continuing games of *Dungeons and Dragons* and *World of Warcraft*, which she plays with other Silicone Valley types, and a sci-fi literature class that she teaches. She has played guitar in her church band.

I love my daughter very much and our relationship is easy. Lisa is a kind, intelligent, and generous person, and I'm very proud of her. Her only fault is that she unabashedly gives to beggars; in fact, she'll go out of her way to find them. I tell her that she's one of the reasons there are so many of those people. She just smiles. It would appear that Lisa has now found some peace, happiness, and fulfillment in her life, and for that I'm grateful.

MEDICAL SCHOOL

Half-awake in Airshipron Two's duty-flight wardroom one afternoon, I overheard two other pilots discussing a previous squadron mate who had taken his MCAT test and applied to medical school while he was still in the squadron. *What a great idea!* So, I did it. Lucky for me, the Navy had a glut of pilots at the time, so they were only too happy to honorably discharge me in November of 1958.

I immediately plunged into the pre-med world of comparative anatomy, embryology, organic chemistry, and the like. Having some mileage behind me, I was finally learning to study and put in the extra effort needed to get those required A's. I organized organic chemistry onto large flow sheets that were more easily memorized, and I almost slept in the embryology department. In the spring of 1959, I got accepted to medical school, which began that fall.

I soon became buried in my studies, sharing a four-hundred-pound cadaver with three other Gross Anatomy lab dissectors. Even though we all worked feverishly during class, our cadaver's immense size made dissection slow—more like mining without dynamite.

Because he had prepared our huge corpse for dissection, and seemed more than interested in how we were progressing, the cadaver manager became one of our best friends. He invited us to see the cadaver tank, where just that morning he had lowered a new body into the formaldehyde-heavy fluid. Several other corpses, stacked in two perpendicular rows, were also submerged in the vaporous liquid. They were being readied for next-year's dissectors. The stench was overwhelming, even for us gross anatomy types, who, we were told, exuded a similar odor throughout the day. You'd think we'd all been swimming in the tank.

Our ageless Gross Anatomy professor, Dr. Hashimoto, was famous for his yearly lecture on the female breast. Using sweeping simultaneous strokes of both hands, he would draw and label the frontal and lateral anatomy of both breasts, in multiple colors—the arteries and veins with his left hand, the ducts and lymphatics with his right. He had an endless supply of jokes and lightened his lectures with mnemonics, such as: "Never Lower Tilly's Pants Mother Might Come Home" (navicular, lunate, triangular, pisaform, greater multangular, lesser multangular, capitate, and hamate bones of the wrist). These memory props were priceless in medical school, and later in practice, but I've wondered how his flamboyant style would play today, women now comprising the majority of most medical school classes. All 55 members of our class were male—my era was indeed "Once upon a time..."

Everyone's bible in pharmacology was *Goodman and Gillman's: The Pharmacological Basis of Therapeutics*...still is. Therefore, Dr. Louis Goodman's yearly, standing-room-only lecture on alcohol was not to be missed. Dr. Goodman would painstakingly describe the physical, mental, social, and societal disasters caused by "that poison alcohol." Then he would pause...and in a deep voice say, "*Stillll*...I can't deny that I've encountered that *rare* person who—for lack of any other explanation—just seems to be one drink below par." This was always followed by explosive laughter from the audience. Comic relief, I guess, after a very disturbing hour.

I sat by my best buddy, Dick Nilson, during most med school lectures, but that was risky. It was best not to call attention to yourself or you might be called upon to answer questions. But trying to be inconspicuous while sitting next to Dick was impossible. He was always whispering comments and observations. Bad enough, but Dick *couldn't* whisper. Dick's whispering was just talking at a lower volume. The lecturer's attention invariably focused on him—and those around him. Most classmates moved away from Dick in lecture amphitheaters, but not me. I just had to resign myself to the fact that, if I chose to sit by Dick, I'd have to be extremely well informed so that I could answer more than my share of questions. Most kids I know can whisper by three years of age. Where did Dick go wrong?

Dick had a large, self-winding wristwatch that had one of the loudest alarms I've ever heard. Amazingly, the alarm's ring seemed to only go off during boring lectures given by professors with no sense of humor. Sleeping fellow students would awaken with a start and Dick would go into a flurry of activity trying to turn the thing off. We all felt like deer in the headlights.

It was chancy to be Dick's friend, but he was the world's nicest guy and an unsurpassed storyteller. Dick's wife, Betty, would laugh at his jokes and stories until the tears came, even though she'd heard them all a thousand times before. As a guy who's been known to tell the occasional lame joke himself, I feel that's a great quality in a woman.

During the clinical rotations, medical students were considered to be slave labor at "County" (Salt Lake County General Hospital). In addition to doing a history and physical examination on each newly admitted patient—at last we got to play doctor—we also had to do the blood drawing (done by phlebotomists or nurses elsewhere) and much of the lab work (done by lab technicians elsewhere). I can still smell the stool samples I had to homogenize in a blender at two o'clock in the morning so I could test them for fecobilinogen. "Scut work" we called it. But we got no sympathy. Our chief of Medicine, Dr. Maxwell Wintrobe (of *Clinical Hematology* fame), felt that because that's the way they'd done it in Boston there was no need to change. We were reminded that medical students in Boston also had to empty bedpans—which we didn't. Thank heaven for small favors, I guess.

When I first started blood drawing, some of my patients cried out in pain, which didn't do much for my self-confidence. But I felt a little better when I saw that it happened to the interns and residents as well. Prompted by a journal article, we looked at some of the offending needles under a microscope and discovered that they had curling burrs of metal at the tip, which must have been painfully tearing much bigger holes in the patient's veins than intended. Obviously, one didn't have to be a craftsman to be a needle sharpener at County. Responding slowly to our complaints, the publicly funded institution eventually allowed us to order those newfangled disposable needles, just recently invented, which essentially ended that form of torture.

Soon after I'd reported for student duty on the VA surgical service, an extremely vocal representative of the Greatest Generation was admitted to have his hemorrhoids surgically removed. On rounds, he let it be known that he only wanted "a hemorrhoid specialist...not some damn resident!" working on his behind. The chief resident replied, with a straight face, "Your lucky, sir, Dr. Rose, a world-renowned hemorrhoid specialist, is making rounds with us today. Dr. Rose, would you please step forward and meet your new patient?"

In my long, freshly laundered white doctor's coat, I played along and examined the guy. "Shouldn't be a problem," I said (I'd seen my first hemorrhoidectomy the day before). But I read everything I could find on the subject that night and did the best I could the next morning, all the while trying to act like the expert he expected.

Hemorrhoid surgery can be pretty painful post-op, but that guy was a trooper and never once complained. He was healing nicely when I saw him in the clinic three weeks later. He thanked me profusely and gave me a box of chocolates. The note inside the box expressed gratitude for my taking his case, as busy as I must have been with my hemorrhoid practice.

For a month during my senior year, I was part of Dr. Peder Lindstrom's neurosurgery team. He was famous for the fact that he had been movie star Ingrid Bergman's first husband, before she ran off with movie director Roberto Rosselini. But, in my book, he was infamous for the then-experimental ultrasonic frontal lobotomies he performed—through wide skull burr holes—on depressed patients. What bothered me most was that he seemed to use the tip of the nose as one of the sighting guides for his free hand procedure. Sighting on a nose the size of mine could easily have produced a blithering idiot, rather than merely a less depressed one.

I had to keep reminding myself that this was the families' last hope for many of these folks. Case in point: I became quite close to one of the patients, an extremely bright man with a severe depressive illness, who freely admitted that he had tried to commit suicide, twice. He had been in the OSS (later the CIA) during WWII and was a particularly valuable asset because he spoke seven languages. He had started, and still owned, a multimillion-dollar business. I enjoyed his quick wit, and joked with him right up till the time the ultrasound machine pulsed his pre-fontal cortex....

Early in the postoperative evening, I noticed a flashing light coming from my patient's room, so I hurried in to see what was going on. He was wide awake, head swathed in bandages and a goofy smile on his face. He was drooling and grunting as he repeatedly inserted and removed a lamp plug next to his bed. He wasn't speaking seven languages anymore. I was told that his psychological affect gradually improved somewhat over the next few months, but I doubt he ever told another joke. Thank God for today's antidepressants.

Toward the end of medical school, it looked as if I would graduate second in the class—a very slow class—so the Dean's secretary pulled out my file one day and said, "Let's see why we accepted you in the first place, Bob." She began scanning the documents. "I don't think it was your architectural ability...very good, but not four point. Maybe your MCAT? Hmmm...well you had been out of school awhile. Good references from Lagoon's Bob Freed, your squadron commanding officer, and Dr. Yamoto but...ahhh...here it is: You had an interview with a University of Utah psychiatry professor, an ex-navy psychiatrist. He said, 'I feel that Lieutenant Rose showed incredibly good judgment when he signed up for the Blimp Corps. I recommend we accept him.' Bob, no one dares argue with a psychiatrist in Utah."

RIGHT TIME AND PLACE

As soon as I got that MD diploma, in 1964, I plunged into a mixed medicine/pediatrics internship at the University of Utah Affiliated Hospitals: Salt Lake County, Primary Children's, and the VA (Veteran's Administration) hospitals. I was now *in charge* and had to ride herd on all of those hopeless medical students. Unfortunately, that assignment also included the dismal task of trying to draw blood from the poor patients the students couldn't—always a challenge after they'd plowed up all of the veins trying. I almost lived at the hospitals. In fact, I eventually did move into the intern's quarters at County. My small and dingy room reminded me of a monk's cell at a monastery, but it didn't matter because I was seldom there.

The Emergency Room was my favorite house-staff rotation. Decisions had to be made fast, and it seemed that my medical judgment improved considerably in County's old primitive ER. After seeing so many brain-splashing motorcycle and motor scooter accidents, I decided to part with my old reincarnated Cushman motor scooter. For the reasonable sum of a hundred and sixty dollars, I replaced that two-wheeled widow-maker with a dirty-green late-1940s Plymouth coupe that had a blue door replacement on the passenger side. Compared to my scooter, it was a moderate step-up in safety (no seat belts) and only slightly warmer in the winter (no heater). But it was infinitely more private, and the dogs couldn't get at me.

Then, like in a Walt Disney movie, I had a magical VA Hospital Neurology Ward moment: I spotted the most beautiful woman I had ever seen. Anne Hansen was a blue-eyed, curvaceous (good Danish genes) nursing student from Richfield, Utah, a Southern Utah town of six thousand souls. As it turned out, Anne had also noticed me when I helped her put hospital pants on old Ralph, one of our bedridden patients with severe MS (multiple sclerosis). Because she thought I was kind to patients, and for whatever other reasons (I presume there were some), she told her fellow nursing students, "I've met the man I'm going to marry."

So her strict nursing instructor wouldn't see us talking, I pushed my uniformed beauty into an elevator and asked her if she would date me in my Green Machine with its cerulean side door? "Yes," she said with such an incandescent smile that I was instantly and hopelessly in love!

We both now remember that our first date was to the movie *Charade,* and that the theme song from that movie was "More," but I had to ask where I'd heard that tune a time or two before I started getting points for remembering. Anne, who had just turned twenty, thinks that I wouldn't have dated her if she had still been nineteen—*wrong!*

The frail neurology patients would smile, or laugh out loud, when I gave Anne a peck on the cheek or a surreptitious pat on her very nice fanny. I discovered that she had interests similar to mine, a great sense of humor, and could put together a great Shepherd's Dinner: a hamburger, potatoes, and onion concoction that she'd wrap in tin foil and cook in the coals of an outdoor fire. When you're smitten, that's a gourmet meal.

Anne's folks, Richard C. and Utahna Hansen, had just gotten over the fact that their daughter was dating a divorced man, ten years her senior, who had a child, when they learned that she was marrying him.

Anne's uncle, David Hansen, married us in the Richfield LDS Tabernacle in the fall of 1964. Following the ceremony, we had a colorful reception at Richfield's Rainbow Café, where Anne had worked as a waitress during high school—probably the reason that I had to repeatedly restrain her from getting up to help clear the tables.

To save money, we had our wedding pictures done in black and white by the hospital morgue photographer, a friend of mine. He seemed happy for the opportunity to do a photo shoot on upright subjects for a change. At least he caught us all with our eyes open.

Dad had a great time at our wedding, repeatedly telling me how happy he was that I'd married Anne. Unfortunately, our wedding was my dad's last major family event. He died of a heart attack three months later, on Anne's twenty-first birthday.

I bought a brand new, aqua-colored 1965 Volkswagen Beetle for our honeymoon trip to San Francisco, selling the Green Machine in the process. Unfortunately, I had left a tennis racket behind the old coupe's front seat that was worth more than the car. On the day of the wedding, we hid the little VW bug in a barn belonging to a friend of Anne's so the car wouldn't be decorated, a Richfield tradition.

Our first night of wedded bliss was spent at Nephi's Safari Motel. We eventually wanted to sleep, but sleep didn't come easily; the Hurricane High School marching band had bought up most of the other motel rooms, so we had sporadic, impromptu concerts for the rest of the night.

Needless to say, we were dog-tired when we arrived in Salt Lake City the next morning for the "mandatory" 300-mile check on our new Volkswagen. As we approached the VW agency, I noticed that the odometer read "299" so I drove around the block twice and arrived with three hundred miles to the tenth. The mechanic said, "Gosh, I don't think I've ever seen a car come in reading exactly 300 miles before." Anne let that one go with no more than a quizzical look.

Then, with a car full of snacks, it was off to San Francisco for a romantic honeymoon, a Fisherman's Wharf presidential campaign speech by Barry Goldwater being a lucky bonus.

We'd saved for a dinner splurge on the last day of our stay and the meal was terrific. Afterward, holding hands in the evening fog, we slowly walked uphill to our new little car that we'd parked under a streetlight on Nob Hill. A clanging cable car had just passed by and the haunting sound of a foghorn could be heard in the distance. I said to Anne, "You know what...?" "What...?" she softly murmured, looking up at me with loving eyes. "I've got to get all of those dead bugs off the hood of that car; the manual says they'll ruin the paint." Sorry, but after three years in the navy, I was a by-the-book man.

Our first home was in the basement apartment of the Church Patriarch's house on the East Bench of Salt Lake City. Our only windows looked out on large sunken window wells that allowed in light but not much of the striking city view. One evening Anne was sitting at the bedroom dresser brushing her hair, her body covered only by a towel. Suddenly, she loudly whispered, *"Bob, someone's up there looking in the window!"*

After telling her to keep brushing, I grabbed a butcher knife, stepped outside into the dark and peered around the corner toward that basement window. Sure enough, someone *was* standing there gazing down at Anne. I shouted, "DON'T MOVE YOU S...O...B!" "Oh dear," said our landlord, "I was just out here checking. I...uh...thought I heard something." I can't blame him. She looked pretty good to me too.

While I worked on my pediatric skills at Primary Children's Hospital, Anne carried a full academic load in nursing and, in our apartment's small kitchen, worked to improve her now-envied cooking skills. On the nights that I could get home, she usually tried out some new dish. Her very first batch of baked biscuits was—let's be honest—tooth-breaking hard. When I couldn't dent one, I looked up and saw that Pooh (my nickname for her) had an anxious look on her face. I playfully heaved the biscuit against the cement wall; it bounced and rolled back across the room without fragmenting. We both broke out laughing.

Though I'd bought Anne her first alcoholic drink (a crème de menthe Grasshopper) on our honeymoon, we were basically both teetotalers. "Half way there," said our church visiting home teacher, who convinced us to pay tithing and such so we could be married in the Mormon temple for time and all eternity. And in the spring of 1965, we were. On the inside of our wedding rings we had engraved "FOR THIS DAY AND ALWAYS," Richard L. Evans' closing phrase at the end of each Sunday morning Mormon Tabernacle Choir broadcast.

Of course, we added to our rings our Richfield wedding date, which was also the date of the Hurricane High School marching band's cacophonous overture that started our new life together.

In June of 1965 we left Utah in our little Volkswagen Beetle and headed to Seattle so that I could become Chief Pediatric Resident at Children's Orthopedic Hospital (now Seattle Children's Hospital). Fortunately, Anne was able to transfer to the University of Washington School of Nursing to complete her training, so we spent almost every weekend I was not on call getting acquainted with Seattle's waterfront, its many parks, the Seattle Center, and the downtown shop windows—anything free or very cheap.

I had helped Dr. Stan Stamm, Chief of Pediatric Cardiology at COH, treat some of his heart patients, so one little girl's grateful parents, commercial fishermen, invited Anne and me to accompany Dr. Stamm, and others involved in their child's care, for a day of offshore Pacific Ocean fishing aboard their family's old trolling (hook and line fishing) boat, aptly named *Adventure*. None of us had been offshore in a boat like theirs, so we didn't realize how large ocean swells could toss about such a tender vessel, or some might have stayed home.

After two hours of being tossed about while attempting to fish, Anne was sick, the captain's wife was sick, and so was nearly everyone else, except the captain and yours truly. Compared to my time on a destroyer in the North Atlantic, it really didn't seem all that bad. I kept fishing, not realizing that others—cursing under their breath—were praying that this adventure would soon end so that we could motor back to the dock.

Then, my first salmon ever seized the line and dove for the bottom. Everyone groaned because they knew this would be no quick fix. I finally worked that big fish up close to the boat and one of my ailing friends tried to help me bring it aboard. But in the process, he vomited all over my soon-to-be Coho salmon meal. Thinking logically, as a scientist, I was sure that cleaning and cooking would neutralize anything objectionable, but that fish still tasted different somehow.

Returning to Seattle from a Christmas trip to Utah, Anne and I drove in snow most of the way. We crossed over Snoqualmie pass at night in a near whiteout blizzard, barely avoiding a collision with a skidding eighteen-wheeler. But as our intrepid little car descended into Western Washington, the snow gave way to light rain, the temperature moderated, and the icy roads disappeared. We looked at each other and nodded—Western Washington was now our home.

KID'S DOC

For two years (1966-1968) I practiced pediatrics in Bellingham, Washington, one year getting in and one getting out. That certainly wasn't the way I'd planned it.

In the university environment, I'd enjoyed caring for sick kids with complicated problems, but in private pediatric practice I probably saw fewer than fifty children a year who really needed a pediatrician. "Parentatrics" more accurately described my practice.

Gladys Finkbonner might make a sobbing evening call to tell me that Stacy was constipated. After I'd suggested prune juice as a remedy she'd wake me up in the middle of the night to tell me "It worked!"

In the 1960s, there were no ER doctors in either of Bellingham's hospitals, so, at any hour of the night, I might be called to an emergency room to see a child whom I'd never seen before, who'd been sick for two or three days, and whose illness had apparently first been noticed by Dad that night after dinner. "Doc, tomorrow's Christmas—he's *got* to be well!" The parents were often furious if I wouldn't prescribe antibiotics for their child's cold and would sometimes refuse to pay my bill.

One memorable evening, Anne and I were giving a dinner party, but I was detained at the hospital to care for a newborn premie. By the time I got home, the guests had finished desert, but they all gathered back around the dinner table so I could be included in their post-dinner conversation. Then...the doorbell rang. I got up from the table and opened the door to see two smiling parents with their arms around their teen-age son. "Dr. Rose," they said, "our son Freddy here needs a physical exam *tonight* so he can play church basketball tomorrow." Whenever I tell this story, people always ask, "Did you do it?"

On another weekend night, I had arranged for pediatric coverage so that Anne and I could have an uninterrupted dinner at a restaurant far out in the county. In the midst of our meal, a sheriff's car drove up to the door with the light-bar flashing. The deputy hurried to our table to inform me that one of my patients was very sick and needed me at the hospital emergency room. When I told the officer that another pediatrician was on call for me, he said, "Yeah, but they don't like him. They want you!" (translation: "We owe him money"). I have no idea how they found out where I was.

A primitive mid-sixties phone system added to our adjustment problems. Even when one of the other two pediatricians was on call, Anne had to answer the phone and explain to patients if they called our home rather than the office's after-hours line. The frequently ringing phone became an enemy in our small apartment. My gut, and Anne's, would turn over when the beast roared at us, day and night. We tried changing the ringer's tone with a paper towel but that didn't help. When I was not on weekend call, we would disconnect the ringer all together, but a residual pre-ring "click" stimulated about as much stomach acid as the original tone. We never got used to it.

But we loved Bellingham. We lived in the Lakeway Apartments, reasonably close to both hospitals and the freeway on ramp. This provided easy access to the Canadian border and Vancouver BC. We gladly paid the Canadians an eight-cent premium on the dollar just to get away from the phone. And to our knowledge, no Mounty ever tried to track down a Bellingham physician at a Canadian restaurant.

Hy's Steak House was our favorite place to dine in Vancouver. We could see our New York steaks, sizzle on the grill in front of us. Like a scene from *Aladdin*, smoke swirled up thickly as the steaks were turned over, but the phantom genie always cleverly escaped through the Hy's subtle overhead ceiling vent.

We seldom drank alcohol so we weren't picky about wine. But when we were at Hy's with friends, we would agree to Sparkling Rose from Kelowna, because it was cheap (reminiscent of Kermit's ordering "Sparkling Muscatel from Idaho" for Miss Piggy in the original *Muppet Movie*).

My eureka moment occurred one morning when I spotted a radiologist friend sitting in St. Luke's Hospital's "X-Ray Department" (Radiology Department everywhere else) reading the Wall Street Journal through his dark adaptive red-lens glasses. He was waiting for his eyes to accommodate to the dark so he could see the screen on the hospital's old non-image-intensified fluoroscope (one of Wilhelm Roentgen's first, I'm sure). Physically drained from running back and forth between hospitals all night playing pediatric emergency room doctor, I flopped down on a chair and said, "How do I join this club, Welde?" Within two days he had me in a four-year radiology residency/fellowship at the University of Oregon Hospital in Portland, Oregon. Our lives changed that fast.

MATT AND FAMILY

The high point of our time in Bellingham was the birth of Matthew Warren Rose in late 1966, at St. Joseph Hospital, a welcome reward for Anne's long and difficult labor. He was a beautiful child, with remarkably long eyelashes, who's picture would have easily won a Gerber baby contest.

I'll tell some short anecdotes about Matt and family, even though many are out of chronologic sequence with the rest of my story.

Matt loved his mom and followed her everywhere. When he was a year old, Anne got a flu-like illness and fell asleep on our bed. She awoke with a start and began frantically looking around for Matt, but he'd just climbed up on a chair by the bed and was noiselessly watching her sleep.

Matthew first saw a mechanical car wash after we'd moved to Oregon. The sudden "wump, wump" of the brushes, the "wap, wap" of the strap roof cleaners, and the deafening "whooosh" of the dryer ("whooper" to Matt) frightened him into an almost catatonic state. Even driving in the same neighborhood as the Lake Oswego car wash produced a fountain of Matt's tears. Clearly, desensitization therapy was in order, so, out of wood, I made a working model of a car wash that Matt could control. Sure enough, after he'd washed his own Tonka cars and trucks a hundred times or so, endlessly repeating the wump...wap...whoosh mantra, he was cured.

Matt was slow to talk but surprised us one day by spontaneously writing "General Electric" on a piece of paper. We realized that he had memorized the label on the refrigerator in the kitchen. For an encore, he wrote "Entering Tualatin" and "Danger—do not go beyond this point," words on signs he'd seen as we'd driven by the Tualatin River. We finally tumbled to the fact that Matt had decreased hearing due to persistent fluid in the middle ear, for which he eventually had ear tubes and tonsil and adenoid surgery. He began talking in complete sentences soon after that.

Matt's special and exclusive relationship with his mother took a real hit when Brad was born. So is it any wonder that one of his first sentences was: "Mom...why don't we take Brad back and get us a *good* baby?" Anne asked, "What's wrong with Brad, Matt?" "He's too big and too *icky*," was the answer.

Matt surprised us by swallowing an unknown quantity of bright-red candy-coated iron pills that he'd grabbed off a high kitchen cupboard shelf we'd thought unreachable. His red stained mouth and fingers were a fortunate giveaway. Luckily, as a pediatrician I'd reviewed the medical literature on this subject because of a similar case, so I knew that iron poisoning was one of the leading causes of death in kids under six. An unobserved ingestion is particularly worrisome. So, though the chief pediatric resident tried to reassure me, "We've pumped all the pills out of his stomach that we can see on X-ray, so he should be OK," I said, "Thanks for doing that, but please do a serum iron level."

Because of the toxic level of iron found in his blood, he was immediately given IV chelation treatment and hospitalized for two days. Because I was working just upstairs, I got to see more of my family than I had for many weeks. Matt's iron levels came down and he was fine, but we'd definitely dodged a bullet.

Four-year-old Matt was standing with his mom on the second deck of the Anacortes ferry, looking aft as we departed Lopez Island. Anne said, "Matt, say bye-bye to Lopez." Young Matt waved and said, "Bye-bye Lopez...Mom, where's Lopez going?"

Matt was delighted when Anne showed him one of those very small Bayer aspirin bottles and told him what it was. "What won't they think of next?" he said.

Five-year-old Matt told his Mom that he wouldn't be able to walk down the block to the babysitter after preschool anymore, because he had to pass by too many barking dogs. Anne said, "Just keep walking, Matt. Don't let the dogs know you're afraid." Matt assured her, "Oh, I'm not afraid...that's not the problem...the problem is [nodding his head] one of them might *kill* me!"

As six-year-old Matt and his brother were about to board the plane to fly to Utah—the first time without us—Anne said, "Now don't worry, Matt. Nanny and Grandpa will be at the airport to pick you and Brad up." Matt said, "They will?" Anne replied, "Yes, Matt. What did you think would happen?" "I guess I thought I'd just call a cab," said Matt.

Our family went to Disneyland for the first time when Matt was eight years old. Only Anne had been there previously, so the rest of us were surprised and amazed. Matt and Brad became best buddies, giggling together as they schemed to slip ahead in those long Disneyland lines. At Knott's Berry Farm, they fine-tuned their techniques. While sitting next to Matt on the plane ride home I noticed that he was crying, so I asked him why the tears? He sobbed, "I'm going to miss Southern California, Dad...I've had such a good time." I thought: *Worth every penny!*

Matt was eight years old when we purchased our family sailboat, *Skye*, and began four years of family sailing, which included some San Juan Islands exploration. At the time, Matt appeared to be only moderately interested in the sailing part, but he loved to row back and forth to shore. In fact, he won the Friday Harbor Lion's Club dinghy race in our old sluggish but safe Sportyak. No small feat.

Matthew was a good athlete when he wanted to be. Ten-year-old Matt won the broad-jump competition in Bellingham's first Arco Jessie Owens Games. The prize was an all-expense paid trip to Los Angeles (including a side-trip to Disneyland) to compete regionally. On Matt's return home, he said, "Dad, you can't believe how long the legs were on some of those kids from LA. They could *step* as far as I could jump."

Both Matt and Brad played youth soccer. I can still remember those cold Saturdays at Battersby Field, the icy wind whistling off nearby Bellingham Bay. Those scantily clad little guys shivered like crazy, even on the sidelines with their coats on. Some goalies would turn a mild hypothermic blue if their team was winning and the action was at the opposite goal. On super cold days, I wore my now-tattered, quilted-down Battersby coat—the warmest I could find—to the games and still froze.

Matt was on Bellingham's select soccer team while he was in high school and was a skillful—though not conservative enough, for my taste—skier. But he eventually became a member of the Mt. Baker Ski Patrol, which saved us considerable ski pass money.

Matt and Brad were sibling rivals. Brad would often get Matt in deep kimchi by provoking him while we weren't looking. Matt would then cuff Brad or get him in a headlock. Brad's pitiful wails, screams, and cries for help would eventually catch our attention and we'd have to respond by punishing the most obvious last offender, usually Matt. It reminded us of a Tom and Jerry cartoon, with Anne or me playing the part of Bertha with the broom.

Startled by a sudden loud rattling of our many overhead windows on Garden Terrace, Anne shouted to the boys downstairs, "WHAT'S GOING ON DOWN THERE?" Matt, sensing an opportunity, quickly shouted back, "I THINK BRAD JUST SLAMMED THE DOOR!" Brad quickly chimed in, "I DID NOT, MATT!" As it turned out, Mt. St. Helens had just blown its volcanic top and the concussive blast had reached us in Bellingham, two hundred miles to the north.

When Matt was in high school, we occasionally paid him to babysit Brad so that we could stay overnight in Seattle or Vancouver. Always the negotiator, Brad convinced us that he would make Matt's job easier if we greased his palm as well. So we gave in and paid him half of the going rate. This system seemed to work fairly well—or so we thought. But several years later, one of the boys' old friends was passing the living room on his way downstairs and remarked, "Hey, this is really a nice room. It was always taped off when I was here before." (not when *we* were home!)

A major advantage of living near the university was that Matt and Brad were welcomed into its congenial computer lab environment. There they learned computer basics and programming in the early days of the digital age. Though we purchased one of the first IBM home computers—complete with Microsoft DOS and a dot matrix printer—both kids preferred the university setting and stimulation. But they'd humor old dad and accompany him to those early PC user clubs. Things were so simple then, before the Internet.

Arcade type video games became the rage when Matt was in high school. Matt's friend's father, a free-wheeling trial lawyer, convinced us that we could start our two boys out on business careers if we bought them three new video machines and put them in the pet shop adjacent to the liquor store in Fairhaven. "High traffic usage," as he put it. This worked for a while, but the boys had a lot of friends, and acquired many *new* friends, all of whom expected free games. Expenses eventually eclipsed revenues and we had to close the operation. I guess, if you don't count the time value of money, we almost broke even. But there's no arguing that something gave Matt an interest in business. We'll pretend it was those three video machines.

Anne and I didn't learn from that experience. We got talked into investing in a lemon farm in Arizona with four other doctors. Year after year, Sunkist reported that our lemons "were so small they could only be used for juice." This meant that we would be paid far less than if they'd been big enough to be sold individually at grocery stores. But finally, someone from our naive investment group visited our farm at harvest time and brought back a few of our lemons, the largest and juiciest we'd ever seen. We absentee landowners were being expertly ripped off.

Matt gave us very few problems in high school, but one doozy stands out. He and his friend, Eric Richardson, loved fireworks. So one Fourth of July they filled our Jeep Wagoneer with a large pile of pyrotechnic bargains they'd bought on the Lummi Indian Reservation and proceeded to set them off at the side of the road. While looking through the unfired heap, still in the car, Matt dropped a lighted punk in the middle of the pile. As you might imagine, all hell broke loose as fireworks began shooting off inside the car. Matt and Eric used their bare hands *(scary!)* to scoop the flaming and exploding mass out of the Jeep and onto the ground—too late for the old Wagoneer, I'm afraid. The interior of the vehicle had been ruined, particularly the car seats and roof. The boys contritely brought the still smoldering vehicle home and showed the disaster to Anne, who said, "Oh my, those seats are really bad." Eric, a future lawyer, replied, "Don't worry, Mrs. Rose. You can get some really fine car seat covers these days."

Matt's four years at the Naval Academy began in the summer of 1985. Suddenly, our boy was being purposely mistreated, a centuries old academy tradition. During the Plebe Summer indoctrination, he lost a lot of weight and was placed on forced feeding. Finally, at the end of his first six weeks at the academy, we were able to visit him, the first time he had been allowed off the grounds. We had planned a big party, but all he wanted to do was come to our hotel room and sleep, unharassed.

I was surprised that Matt selected offshore sailboat racing as his major sport at the academy, but he must have been soaking it up as we sailed Skye, and he raced with others, on Bellingham Bay. He became a forty-foot yacht skipper and won several trophies for Navy's offshore racing fleet. He told me that one of the reasons he went out for sailing, rather than soccer, was he thought the competition for a varsity soccer position would be fierce, but "How many guys from places like Kansas can sail?"

Matt's Naval Academy graduation in 1989 was a once-in-a-lifetime event. There were three days of pageantry, including two close-up performances by the navy's Blue Angels. They flew low over the Severn River in their new, blue F18 Hornets as we sat spellbound on the adjacent drill field grass. One of the planes even slowed above the water just in front of us and seemed to balance vertically on its twin tail exhausts before its afterburners kicked in and it roared up out of sight. Standing in the very hot sun at the graduation ceremony, then Secretary of Defense Cheney handed out the diplomas, and the hats were in the air!

With a degree in aerospace engineering, Matt began training to be a naval aviator, which included obligatory jet plane landings on the canted-deck carrier *Lexington*. After he got his wings, he flew P3 Orion four-engine sub-hunting/electronic surveillance aircraft for the remainder of his ten-year active-duty career, and for three years in the naval reserve. He began flying Boeing 737's for United Airlines in September of 1999 but, sensing that United was in trouble after the 9/11/2001 terrorist attacks on the World Trade Center and the Pentagon, he took a leave of absence to enter graduate school at Harvard. This proved to be a wise move because he was later furloughed from United as part of a reduction in force of more than 2,100 pilots.

Sarah Briggs was Matt's most incredible piece of luck. He met this beautiful and intelligent woman, with a great sense of humor, on a dock in Bermuda after the Naval Academy yacht he was skippering finished the Newport to Bermuda race. Sarah's dad was crewing on a boat that had just completed the same race, so she was there to greet him. Over the next few years, while Matt was pursuing his Navy flying career and Sarah was in school, they fell in love and were eventually married in Boston in the summer of 1994.

Anne and I hosted a memorable wedding rehearsal dinner at Mamma Maria, an Italian Restaurant near the Paul Revere House. The next day the bride and groom were married in military style at Boston's stately Church of the Advent. The wedding guests were then transported by trolley back to the Harvard Club, where the out-of-towners were staying, for a lavish Briggs' reception. I made an ass of myself trying to protect my niece Julie from a guy named Rick, whom I had seen making out with various women on the bachelor party tour of bars. I guess that no one but me thought Julie needed protecting.

Sarah is Matt's rudder. She is thoughtful, cheerful, artistically talented, a great cook, and a fine gardener. In fact, before moving on to the construction business, she had her own successful landscaping company. She has good judgment and incredible child-rearing and people skills. We're extremely fortunate that our son met Sarah.

Katherine Elaine Rose (Sweetface), the first of our two beautiful granddaughters, was born in Pensacola in the summer of 1998, an unbelievable smiling, gurgling gift.

Kate talked early and chattered continually. She was an early reader, thanks to Sarah's tireless efforts to expose her to the library and the world of books. It soon became apparent that she was a talented artist, constantly drawing and creating all manner of artwork, which eventually included glue-gun animal sculptures made of rocks, shells, and other small objects she found on our Lummi Island beach.

Kate substituted the y-sound for l's until she was three years old. Sucking on a piece of lime that I had just given her, she rushed over to Anne on the couch and said, "Grandma, I just yuv yemmons and yimes." Six months later, no longer substituting y for l, she ordered lunch at Lummi Island's Beach Store Café, "I'll have a bowl of crab and a bowl of vanilla ice cream, please." About the same time, she named our one-step-down utility room "the basement"

Grandma taught Kate to identify the United Airlines name on brochures and other written material while we were waiting to board a plane in the Honolulu airport. That went pretty well, so, to impress the gate agents as we were boarding, Gram pointed to a big banner with the company name and logo on it and said to her precocious granddaughter, "Kate, what does that say?" Kate puffed herself up and shouted, "KATHERINE ELAINE ROSE!"

Four-year-old Kate's Beanie Baby cat was her constant companion. She said, "I know that Pounce is real because if I put food out for him, when I'm not looking, he eats some of it." Indeed, Pounce has been reincarnated several times and is still an important part of our lives, surreptitiously showing up when least expected. One Christmas, Kate awakened to find Pounce—then missing for months and presumed lost—peering out from her Christmas stocking. Beanie cat in hand, Kate turned around and matter-of-factly said, "See, I told you Pounce'd come home for Christmas."

At five, Kate asked her mom if she could go out to play. Sarah replied, "You can't go outside, Kate, it's raining." "Mom, it's not raining...it's just *water*!"

Six-year-old Kate told Grandma, "Things are good for me right now: I'm the biggest girl in my class, I have a loose tooth, and I have a horse [stick horse]."

In 2006, the Catholic Church was selecting a new Pope and the process was being exhaustingly covered by television news. Kate was fascinated by the event and eventually asked, "What's happening, Grandma?" After Grandma, to the best of her knowledge, had explained the election procedure, Kate excitedly said, "Oh Grandma, I hope they choose Warren [her brother]."

Eight-year-old Kate was encouraging Grandma to get a dog. "What kind of dog would you want, Gram?" Grandma replied that she'd probably want a lab if she had a big house and a dachshund if her house was small. Kate said, "Oh Gram, you should get a Corgi—they don't care what size house they live in."

Another time, Kate asked, "What's your thing, Gram?" Grandma answered, "I don't know what you mean, Kate." Kate said, "Well, Gramp has lots of strawberries in his patch but he said that we couldn't eat any more of them until you'd done your *thing*."

Kate and I looked for agates and sea glass on our first beach walks. But she soon began picking up and examining tiny crabs we found under rocks and catching small eels on very low tides. These and other critters eventually became the purpose of our walks, which before long included her brothers.

Kate, now a young woman, is currently attending Tulane University on a merit scholarship. She is an artist, a published short story writer, an honors violinist, an 800 meter and cross-country runner, an exceptional skier, and a natural-born leader. I love her and am very proud of her.

In 1999, Matt and Sarah moved back to Bellingham, eventually buying a house on North Forest St. Matt was still flying for United Airlines at the time my first grandson, Spencer, joined our family.

Spencer Joseph Rose (Spenceman) was born in the summer of 2000 at Bellingham's St. Joseph Hospital, where his dad was also born and where I spent so many of my working years.

Spence is a very handsome and precocious first grandson who has a quick wit, a big smile, and his dad's long eyelashes. He's going to be tall, perhaps six-foot-three or so, says my brother Pat, the pediatrician. A size fourteen shoe at fifteen years of age helps support Pat's prediction.

One of Spence's early words was "bananananinas," which his two-year-old cousin Gus thought was "a really good one" when Grandma told him about it a few years later.

Two-and-a-half-year-old Spencer woke me up early one morning, pushed up my sleep mask, and asked, "Grandpa...are you pretending to be a dog?" At about the same age, Spence shouted at his other grandma, Susan's, incessantly barking miniature Collie: 'ENOUGH, SHACK!'" The mimic of Susan's voice was right on.

In the fall of 2003, we celebrated Anne's dad's 90th birthday in a hotel across the street from Temple Square in Salt Lake City. The next morning, Anne, the Matt Rose family, and I walked over to watch and hear the Mormon Tabernacle Choir perform their weekly Sunday morning television broadcast. As we entered the tabernacle, an obviously impressed Spencer asked one of the ushers, "Is this the castle with the singers?"

Always the kind diplomat, four-year-old Spencer came home from Montessori school reporting that he had painted a picture of a sunset. "It must have been beautiful," said Sarah. "It *was* beautiful. But you know, Mom, Remington just drew a black scribble...or maybe it was a cave with no bears?"

Spencer spent countless hours studying the pictures in the books that had been endlessly read to him, but when he was five years old he began reading those books—and everything else for that matter. Alas, Anne and I had to stop spelling out loud in front of him.

Once, Spencer was sucking on some cake candles at a birthday party, so Grandma said, "Oh no, Spencer, don't chew on those candles." Spencer sternly replied, "Grandma, at our house we have our own rules—we eat birthday candles!"

That same year, Grandma said, "Spence, I brought you a little something from Hawaii. Spencer retorted, "Grandma, don't use that word with me. A *little* something sounds like not much at all."

Six-year-old Spencer asked Grandma why we do so many things for Jesus' birthday. Grandma said, "Because he's the son of God, Spencer." Spence replied, "What? You've *got* to be kidding! Now that's *really* something!"

When Spence's Uncle Brad and Aunt Bonnie first found out that they were going to have a baby girl we were all sitting around thinking about possible names for the little sweetie. Suddenly, Spence giggled and said, "Hey, you could name her Hairball. Look everybody—Hairball just took her first step."

A somewhat older Spence left his clothes all over the floor of the back bedroom before climbing into bed. I said, "Spence, pick up those clothes. Do you think you're a snake and can drop your skin anywhere?" Without a pause Spence replied, "Gramps, that poor snake probably doesn't have a grandpa to remind him."

Twelve-year-old Spencer answered the phone when Grandma called their home from Hawaii. She asked him how the family was doing. "Well, Gram, the way I see it, we're all just regular people living ordinary, everyday lives."

Looking up from a book he was reading, Spence said, "I agree with this: '*Nothing* is sometimes the best thing to do.'" Warren observed, "Well, that's good because you do that *best thing* quite often."

As they were for me, comics are a big deal for Spencer. But he doesn't have to rely on under-the-bed boxes of comic magazines as I did. After a visit from Spence, my online log usually shows that he's seen one heck of lot of cartoons in a little bit of time. I'd have loved that as a kid.

Spence has a photographic memory and seems to never forget anything. He loves history and geography and once told me that, when he grew up, he wanted to be a paleontologist: "Gramp, I'm really into dinosaurs." He's a thespian (*The Music Man*), a debater (says he might want to be a lawyer), and a good skier. He can strike up an animated conversation with anyone and can sing (Sehome Chamber Choir and

Oliver Warbucks in *Annie*) and whistle. We used to whistle together, a real treat for me. I'd love to do a YouTube movie of that someday. I'm sure it'd go viral. I love Spence and am very proud of him.

In the summer of 2002, Matt became a student at the Kennedy School of Government and the business school at Harvard University while he worked on a Master of Public Administration degree. The family lived with Dick and Susan Briggs, who retreated to an attached apartment and allowed the Roses to occupy the whole four-bedroom upper level of their Winchester, Massachusetts home. As welcome guests, Anne and I got to be a part of our grandkid's lives when we visited, including that of our second grandson, Warren.

Warren Philip Rose ("Squeedunk") was born in Boston Massachusetts in the summer of 2002. I wouldn't have believed that we could have another brilliant and good-looking grandchild, but we did. None of that "goo" and "coo" stuff for Warren; his first semi-word at ten months of age was a low-pitched "budda-budda-budda," imitating the sound of large trucks or busses passing by. He nodded and said "Ga" for yes at one year of age...so cute. Even after he could say yes, he was slow to give it up because he knew we all loved it.

Warren talked very early. He had two loquacious siblings, so he had to. When he was two-and-a-half-years old, he said, "Grandma, why you don't have a mom and dad?" Grandma replied, "I have a dad who is very old, but my mom is dead." "Oh," he said and then walked off. Much later he came back and said, "Grandma, who killed your mom?"

During Christmas service at St. Paul's Episcopal church, Grandma whispered to Warren, "I think I hear hoof beats on the roof.... It must be Santa and his reindeer." Warren was beside himself with that joyful news. A few months later, while sitting in the same church pew awaiting baptism, Warren whispered to Grandma, "I think I hear someone on the roof.... It must be Jesus."

That would have been the time to baptize the boy. But the powers-that-be turned what should have been a short baptismal service into a two-and-a-half-hour pomp and circumstance event before getting down to business. By then, Warren was exhausted. As they hauled him up in front of the whole congregation to be sprinkled, he screamed, "I DON'T WANT TO BE BAPTISED, I *HATE* IT!" While he was stepping down, someone must have said, "Now that was OK, wasn't it?" because he shouted out, "NO—I *HATED* IT!" So much for that.

While camping in the Cascades with his family, on the way to Chelan, almost-four-year-old Warren accompanied everyone out to see if they could spot a fox that Matt had noticed while he was jogging. After apprehensively looking around for a while, Warren said, "I hope that fox doesn't bite me...then I won't have to kill his whole family!"

Soon after that, Grandma told Warren that she loved him. He replied, "You don't love me Grandma. Grandpa loves me." "But I love you too, Warren!" "No Grandma...just Grandpa."

Just before Christmas, Anne had barely walked into Village Books bookstore when she heard a little voice to her left shout, "WHAT THE HELL ARE *YOU* DOING HERE?" —Warren, of course. The kids were there with their godparents, John and Martha, picking out their Christmas presents.

On a home video that same Christmas, Warren was heard saying, "I disappointed Duck (his small security blanket with a simulated duck's head) when I told him he couldn't have a gun for Christmas. I don't want guns in the house! But if he grows up and wants to hunt, I will buy him a gun." Later, he told us that Duck "jumped off infinity cliffs."

During a phone call, four-year-old Warren told me that he was getting over a cold so I asked if he was feeling better. Off-phone, I heard him ask, "Mom, am I feeling better?"

Noticing Warren standing on the bathroom scale in her closet, Grandma asked him what he was doing? He said, "I just want to see how tall I am."

At Campbells Resort in Chelan, this same guy, now five years old, ran by us at the tail end a gang of kids. He shouted out, "WE'RE JUST LOOKING FOR BOMBS AND DEAD BODIES!"

While at Aunt Jane's house in Las Vegas, Warren asked, "Where's that lady who looks like Grandma and cooks?" He then added, "I'll have French toast."

On the day Spencer learned to ride his bike at Lummi Island, all of the family was out by the road making a fuss over him. Kate, Spencer, and Warren, with his training wheels, had just biked down to Lane Spit Park and were racing back. Suddenly, Spencer and Kate collided and went down hard. Trailing Warren kept vigorously riding. He soon passed the tangled wreck and wheeled up to Grandma. "Well...I guess I won *that* race."

Five-year-old Warren was telling his mom how much he liked the morning playschool at the YMCA. "Mom, I really like the swimming and—please don't tell Spencer—I like talking to the girls too."

Warren was sitting on the top step of Cambells' hot tub, surrounded by several silent and seemingly bored older kids. After a quiet moment, Warren looked up at the kids and said, "Have you ever been stung by a bee...?" There was a collective "Yeaaah," and suddenly the kids were talking to Warren, and each other, all caught up in the magic of the moment. I believe you call that a facilitator.

Kindergarten-age Warren told Grandma that four times four was sixteen. When she asked him how he knew that, he replied, "I just see it in my head, Gram."

Later, six-year-old Warren did an "Eeny, meeny, miny, moe" and "My mother told me" trying to decide between two Haagen-Dazs bars at the Islander store. On our ride home, he said, "Grandpa, I *really* wanted that dark chocolate bar that I got; that's why I started with Eeny on the other one." I asked him if anyone had told him that or if the any of the other kids had figured it out (I hadn't). He answered "no" to both questions. Then, I asked him if he had a plan for three bars. "I'm working on that," he said.

Kate saw eight-year-old Warren wearing a helmet and carrying a shield during a water fight. When she asked him why, he said, "Kate, sometimes life gets complicated."

When I asked ten-year-old Warren how he was going to count the large number of hits in a target's bull's-eye he'd shredded using my old iron-sight pump twenty-two rifle, he said, "I'll just count those that aren't bull-eyes and subtract that from the number of shots I fired." Why didn't I think of that? There weren't many misses.

Warren has an engineer's mind; while in the fourth grade he built a detailed eco-friendly house ("green" roof, water recirculation, solar panels, etc.) and a catapult model that really worked. He's fascinated with weaponry, remote controlled aircraft, and robots. But being in a university modern dance group performance at the Firehouse Theater helped him reveal his creative side, and being elected eighth-grade president showed his political nature. He's an excellent tennis player, and, like his siblings, Warren can ski. I love him and am very proud of him

Soon after the Harvard and Kennedy School graduation ceremonies, the Matt Rose family moved to Celebration, Florida while Matt was working on a startup company with a business school friend. Celebration was fun for all of us, but why wouldn't it be? It was a planned part of the Disney World complex. We had some good times in the swimming pool and at the nearby Magic Kingdom. The live alligator in the city-center lake was an interesting touch. It was while visiting the family at Celebration that I first realized I was getting older: I had to roll to my hands and knees before I could get up from one of their ubiquitous blowup floor mattresses.

We're fortunate that the Matt Rose family has returned to Bellingham. After a few years as Operations Director for Northwest Radiologists, Matt became part-owner of a water management company, Apana, that is helping businesses like Costco reduce their water costs.

Matt has given us some great moments. He is a bright, moral person who is a leader in the community, serving on several boards and commissions. He toys with the idea of one day running for public office. I love him very much and am proud of him. I thank him for marrying Sarah. Their combined parenting skills have thus far produced three happy, delightful, and well-adjusted kids who have a lust for life.

X-RAYS AND STUFF

To add excitement to our four-year University of Oregon radiology residency adventure, we bought our first house, a four-bedroom rambler in Lake Grove, a newer but more humble part of the affluent Portland suburb of Lake Oswego. Our fenced-in lot had five big, beautiful fir trees in one corner, two large rocks for the kids to climb on, and a third of an acre of lawn for Anne to mow.

We had access to a nearby gated picnic park that provided opportunities for swimming, boating, and Fourth of July fireworks on Oswego Lake, still claimed by many Oregonians to be the birthplace of waterskiing in the United States (a fact hotly disputed by Lake Pepin Minnesotans). This first home cost $19,000. When we left Lake Grove in 1972, we sold the house for $26,000, thinking we'd made a killing. With another bedroom added, it was worth $401,000 in 2016. Keep in mind that salaried incomes were much less in 1968, and interest rates were high.

The faculty of the University of Oregon's Department of Radiology consisted of the most colorful characters you could imagine. The chairman, Charles T. Dotter MD, was an admittedly asocial genius who almost single-handedly developed the basic techniques for maneuvering catheters and other invasive interventional devices (i.e., special needles, tubes, and various other inserts) through blood vessels or into body cavities, organs, and what not, for which he was nominated for the Nobel Prize in medicine in 1978. With that said, if you stopped by the genius's home on an errand, he would often have to kick a pile or two of doggie doo out the way to let you in, if he decided to let you in at all.

Charlie was a serious mountain climber who often went climbing with Dr. Marsha Bilbao, the director of resident training, an unusual character in her own right. Many residents suspected that they might have been having an affair, but I couldn't believe that. "Nope...they're both odd enough that it just *ain't* happening," I repeatedly testified, and I'm still sure I was right.

Charlie and Marcia gave their best combined performance at a dinner sponsored by a medical equipment company. The dinner, which was for residents and their spouses, was held at one of Portland's best hotels. Near the end of the main course, each of our two mentors retrieved a large leashed dog from their car. Then they proceeded to go down both sides of the table, encouraging the animals to clean off the guest's plates, whether they had finished eating or not. One of the wives tried to quickly gobble down the remains of her steak, but she soon surrendered it when faced with bared fangs and a menacing growl.

Cigar-smoking, bow-and-arrow-bear-hunting Louis Frische MD was professor of Gastrointestinal Radiology. Lou had become wealthy when the value of the gold he had hoarded for years surged from $35 to $400 an ounce, as the government's fixed price for the commodity was terminated. To see the frugal way that Lou lived and dressed you'd never have guessed that he was a well-heeled multi-millionaire. Ultraconservative, crew-cut Lou was a longtime vociferous member of the NRA and the John Birch Society, the virtues of which he often extolled.

Lou reviewed all of the day's fluoroscopy cases in a small, crowded, poorly-ventilated room that he ceaselessly filled with cigar smoke. Because of this irritating cloud, the X-ray films were difficult to see, but Lou could pick out an overlooked ulcer with ease. His mantra at every session was "Buy gold," as he ranted that the economic system was about to collapse. His advice was lost on his audience of residents, none of whom had any money.

Lou liked to go four-wheeling on his bear hunts. He was actually delighted to get stuck in the mud and snow so far back in the woods that he had to winch his vehicle out. He loved to brag about these escapades and would occasionally invite some of us along. On one of these hunts, Lou, seated on a stump, stabbed a hunting knife into his left quadriceps muscle as he tried to impale a steak balanced on his thigh. He had forgotten for the moment that it was on a paper plate. None of us reacted or mentioned it to him later because no one wanted to embarrass this truly good guy, great teacher, and undisputed woodsman of the world. Knowing Lou was well worth the one or two years his second-hand smoke might have shortened my life.

The motto of most general radiology programs was: "See a procedure—do one—teach one." However, in our institution it was usually: "Just do one—don't be a sissy—and [except for Lou Frische] don't look for help." Our general radiology department faculty was only randomly involved, so we residents tried to help train each other whenever possible. We became very resourceful.

In angiography and invasive interventive procedures it was a different story. We had some of the finest teachers in the world: Joseph Roesch in general angiography, Mel Judkins in corony angiography, Vince Hinck in neurologic angiography, and, of course, Charles Dotter in peripheral vascular and invasive procedures. They were all pioneers in their fields and gave us an excellent foundation in these new techniques.

After we had moved back to Bellingham, Charlie and Marcia paid us a visit. They were planning to hike over the Cascades to Stehekin at the Northwest end of Lake Chelan, where Lou Frishe would pick them up in his seaplane and fly them back to Portland. After taking them around town to get the equipment and supplies they needed, I dropped them off at the trailhead and forgot about it. Months later, I received a dramatic photograph of Charlie hanging out into thin air, suspended by a safety line belayed to a stone crag. This was a picture I had seen on the wall of his office and had always coveted. I must have told him so. The photo was accompanied by a small piece of granite rock and a note: "This stone is from the top of the Matterhorn. Thanks, Bob!"

Our social life usually involved our fellow radiology residents and their spouses. Anne and I hosted Halloween party spectacular for the group. We pushed our living room furniture into the garage, tossed all of the furniture cushions on the floor, hung Halloween colored crepe paper nets and balloons from the ceiling and walls, filled the room with eerie light, and played moody music to greet the arriving costumed guests. Two large round pumpkins won the costume prize—no close dancing there. Everyone seemed to have such a great time that one inebriated couple actually dropped by the next weekend, hoping they might find us throwing another party, I kid you not.

Gerry Johnson (one of the two pumpkins mentioned) invited Gil Cordova, George Burgermeister, and me to go fishing with him on the Columbia River Bar, a stretch of water at the mouth of the Columbia River that can be very treacherous for a small boat like Gerry's. Fortunately, it was a calm, foggy day and there was minimal wind to conflict with the current. I caught our only fish, a forty-pound Chinook (king) salmon, technically a "Tyee" (thirty pounds or greater). The guys never let me forget that I made them stop every few miles on the way back to Portland so I could pour water over that big fish, which was lying exposed in the back of the Gerry's pickup truck. There was no way I was going to let that mega-salmon dry out and shrink before I could show it to Anne, the kids, and all the neighbors.

I was an usher in Gil and Sharon Cordova's wedding party. I guess they felt they needed some muscle. Gil got wind of some shenanigans being planned for the bride and groom's nighttime departure, so he asked me to drive the get-away car. Apparently he forgot to tell Sharon, who, escaping her rice throwing pursuers, jumped onto the front passenger seat just as Gil leapt into the back. I gunned out of there in the darkness, whereupon Sharon settled back, grabbed my thigh, and began massaging it. As we passed under a streetlight, she wistfully looked over at me, her eyes widened, and she gasped, "Oh my...!"

Anne and I took a backpacking and camping course at Portland's OMSI (Oregon Museum of Science and Industry), so we could camp with our friends. We learned how to pack a backpack with camping essentials but still keep it ultra-light, using layered synthetic clothing, freeze-dried foods, and ultra-small fluid bottles. We were given other helpful ideas like cutting off half of our toothbrush handles to keep the weight down. Heeding our teachers' advice, we arrived at the trailhead with only the bare essentials for our first post-class hiking and camping trip with the Johnsons and the Cordovas, both couples experienced campers.

Our camping buddies were responsible for dinner. They were a little late because they had stopped at the store to get steaks, baking potatoes, corn, and wine. Because the hike in was about six miles, we were a little taken aback at the menu choices. But we accepted our share of the added weight and somehow made it up the steep trail to the campground (we were young then). After dinner that night, we happily slipped into our sleeping bags, both agreeing that our pals certainly knew how to camp.

Another friend, Dewey Matthews had been a well thought of family practitioner before he joined our radiology resident ranks. Dewey was capable and likeable, a natural leader, and a John Wayne kind of guy. After weeks of watching Dewey for flaws, the only thing we came up with was that he washed his hands *before* he used the urinal, not after.

Being almost perfect eventually took its toll on Dewey. While giving Anne and me a tour of a large log house he'd personally built for his family, he kept pointing out minor errors he'd made, which none of us could see. When our tour arrived at a big beautiful stone fireplace and chimney he'd constructed at one end of the high-ceilinged living room, I finally said, "Dewey, this is awesome—please spare us the screw ups lecture." Dewey smiled, apparently relieved, and told us where he'd gotten the stone and how much fun he'd had building the fireplace. I've tried to learn from this but I sometimes find myself "doing a Dewey," as we used to call it.

One of Dewey's rare blunders was his choice of a gigantic Bullmastiff to be the family dog on his small farm. The mastiff was a gentle, but not too bright, animal that would soak your pants with his juicy jaws when he welcomed you, particularly if you were sitting down and couldn't ward him off.

"Brutus" hated the family cat, which had scratched his nose when they'd first been introduced. Because the big dog had frequently trashed the house while chasing the feline, Dewey chained him to a cast iron heat radiator in the living room. Knowing that Brutus was tethered, kitty would taunt him by prancing back and forth, just out of reach. But one day, the cat did one prance too many as he paraded on the living room window sill, just two feet from the huge dog's nose. "Enough!" said the massive canine's relatively small brain, and Brutus performed a colossal lunge that snapped the radiator from the floor. Then, in a cloud of steam, the enormous dog, the chain, and the clanging heater crashed through the window and were last seen plowing up the vegetable garden, close on the heels of the panicked and fleeing tabby.

Dewey's neighbors, two elderly poultry-raising women, complained that Brutus was chasing their chickens, so Dewey chained the dog to a stout outside clothesline. Unsurprising to everyone but Dewey, Brutus soon broke loose and was missing for an hour or two before he came loping home, two chicken feet protruding from one side of his mouth. A very sad Dewey pried open the dog's massive jaws to retrieve a wet and lifeless chicken, which was placed on the ground while Brutus was chained to a thick post. As Dewey was about to pick up the bird for burial, one of its eyes popped open, it let out a loud squawk, and then, wings a-flapping, it scampered home to the neighbor ladies' chicken coop.

That residency time in Oregon was a great interlude. Many summer days were spent picnicking at the community easement on Lake Oswego or trekking the Portland Zoo, where young Matt seemed more interested in cranking the drinking fountains on and off than observing the animals. Maybe his time piloting OMSI's (Oregon Museum of Science and Industry) retired old DC-3 airplane, with little Brad as his copilot, helped determine some of Matt's early career choices.

Our frequent trips to the Oregon Coast were usually good, cheap fun, but on one scary outing we almost lost Matt and Brad to a rogue wave while they were playing on the beach near Astoria. Anne first noticed that the ocean had receded from the rusty skeletal remains of the *Peter Iredale* shipwreck, but she soon saw a big wave rolling in. She frantically grabbed Brad and threw him up behind a partially buried log. Matt, further out on the beach, for once came running when Anne called, and she barely pulled him to safety as the large wave hit. Fortunately, some folks on the bluff above saw what was happening and jumped down to help rescue Brad, who was half submerged in a pool of water behind the log. Rogue waves claimed several lives on Oregon's shores that year, but fortunately not ours. We spent the afternoon at the Astoria Laundromat, drying our clothes.

When my neuroradiology fellowship was completed, we borrowed $2,500 from a local bank, bussed a trusted babysitter down from Bellingham, and took a three-week South Pacific vacation in those wonderful days before Boeing 747s. We first flew to Tahiti, sitting just behind the cargo net on an uncomfortably multipurpose French airliner. Then we spent a few days each in Tahiti's Moorea and Bora Bora, Fiji's Toberua Island, Auckland, New Zealand, Sydney, Australia, and Pago Pago, American Samoa. To make the trip painless, we had drivers pick us up from the airports and take us where we needed to go. I have no idea how our travel agent did it for that price, though it seemed a lot of money at the time.

Hotel Bora Bora and its reef-protected lagoon were so beautiful that Anne, wearing no protective T-shirt or effective sunscreen, snorkeled her way to a sick sunburn. She missed a whole day's activities, which included two French gourmet meals on our Modified American Plan hotel accommodations. Because the meals were already paid for, I tried to eat her share and have enough fun for both of us…when I wasn't looking in on her, of course

The Toberua Hotel was on a private Fiji island that could only be reached by taking a boat from the larger island of Viti Levu. Accompanying us on our boat trip was Darren McGavin, star of stage, screen, and TV (*The Christmas Story* movie and two Wikipedia pages of other credits), and his actress wife, Kathie Browne. Anne was indeed star-struck. As we approached the island's dock, we could see that a large group of islanders had gathered. Darren shook his head and said, "Oh, I wish they wouldn't do that. We'd just like to be treated like everyone else." Then we disembarked and a village elder asked, "Who is Dr. Rose?" When I identified myself, the villagers picked up our bags and led us to the nicest bure on the island, leaving Darren and Kathie standing by their luggage with their eyes wide and mouths open.

As it turned out, the island folks couldn't get reliable medical care from the doctors on the big island. Most of those docs were of minority East Indian decent, whom the native Fijians accused of practicing fratricide by neglect (one of several factors that eventually led to unrest and revolt in Fiji). So…I held sickbay for the islanders. Quite pleasant, actually, and very much appreciated. Most of the patients had infected coral wounds that they'd gotten catching fresh seafood for our meals. When I asked how they'd get the needed antibiotics if I prescribed them, the hotel manager said, "Write down what we need, Dr. Rose. It won't be easy, but I'll get it."

Our bure on Tomberua was certainly South Sea sumptuous, but termites liked the bamboo edifice as much as we did. We could hear them chomping away in the middle of the night, their gnawing amplified by the bamboo's tubular structure…like pipes on an organ. We made the mistake of mentioning the sound to the manager on our way to breakfast, and we returned to find our room filled with green nerve gas that we could only hope was of insect dosage. Even with the large louvered windows and doors wide open, it was not until late afternoon that we could reenter our room safely. In spite of the poisonous cloud, we had a termite concert reprise that evening, perhaps even louder, in protest. We sucked it up and said nothing.

We had several meals with the McGavins, who were good folks. We learned that Darren was actually William Lyle Richardson from Spokane, Washington (go figure). We loved it when an Aussie sheep rancher having dinner with the McGavins and us said to Anne: "Now I would guess that *you're* the movie star?" Kathie was quick to correct that impression.

The highest elevation of Toberua island was only a few feet above sea level, so it's no wonder that some sea beasts would find their way ashore. I saw the pool boy carrying a long black-and-white ringed snake from the pool area, his hand wrapped tightly around the reptile's neck. "Don't worry, sir. It's not poisonous," he assured me. An article in the hotel's National Geographic Magazine collection corrected that misinformation, confirming that sea snakes are "highly venomous." So when my big toe was agonizingly grabbed by something hiding on the bottom of the hotel's pool, I thought it was surely a sea snake and that I was about to die. But a moderately sized dark-shelled crab, hiding on a black line, proved to be the culprit--- still hurts to think about it.

Three unique experiences worth mentioning occurred after we left Fiji: a taxi driver in Rotorua, New Zealand offered to buy us a pint at his local pub as he drove us home to our hotel from the Maori Carving School; some kind New Zealanders saw us "Yanks" (we must have been obvious) at a bus stop in Auckland and invited us to come home with them and have Sunday dinner; and an enormous Samoan woman sat down next to Anne on a bus and began stroking her hair, all the while looking straight ahead, expressionless. Anne, her eyes wide, didn't move a muscle. After a few minutes, the bus stopped, the woman exited without a glance or word, and Anne started breathing again.

Before heading back to Bellingham to join the radiology group, we visited our families in Utah. My brother Nick weighed in, "You can't go into practice looking like that!" He promptly took me to his clothier in Salt Lake City, where he picked out a fashionable wine-colored polyester suit, complete with light-gray lapel and pocket stitching and bell-bottom pants. Two paisley-patterned polyester dress shirts, two broad, paisley polyester ties, and a wide, tooled leather belt completed my new wardrobe. After I gave up my crew cut for an Elvis look, I felt like the grandest tiger in the jungle and was more than ready for the big move.

I'd bought a unicycle in the last year of residency and had spent countless hours hanging onto a clothesline while I learned to ride it. Finally, I was able to unsteadily pedal out of our driveway, into the street, and back, quite an accomplishment, I thought. Then our moving van arrived and one of the movers said, "I always wanted to try one of these things." After he effortlessly balanced himself on my one-wheeled device, he rode it down the driveway and up a ramp into his large van, as if it was the easiest thing in the world to do.

BRAD AND FAMILY

Hugh Bradford Rose was born in Portland, Oregon, in late 1969. Once again, Anne had a long, difficult labor that ended with Brad being delivered by low forceps. This resulted in some bleeding under the outer covering of his skull's right parietal bone (cephalohematoma). The trauma was innocuous, but, as is usual for the condition, blood ossifying about the periphery of the bone during healing left Brad with what feels like a dent in his head, but isn't. Kids think it is; they love to feel it.

Now I'll tell a few anecdotes about Brad and family, even though many are out of sequence with the rest of the story.

Brad was an active, loveable baby, but at two years of age, congenial "Sparkle" started a cry/flop-in-the-middle-of-the-grocery-store-aisle routine you just had to admire. As suggested by Dr. Spock in his classic book, Anne would leave him alone on the floor while she anxiously peered around the end of the aisle waiting for the episode to end. It always did, of course, as suddenly as it had begun, like flame-spouting baby Jack-Jack in *The Incredibles* movie.

Two-and-a-half-year-old Brad, white hair awry, was wearing a pair of bib overalls and a red-and-white-striped shirt when he fell down and skinned his nose. As Anne held up still sniffling Brad to let him see his red nose in a mirror, he gasped, "I'm tasting like a clown!"

At three or four years of age, our "Spark" stood on the sidewalk in front of our home and called across the street to his sometimes-babysitter, Chris Hamilton, to take his hand so he could cross the road and visit. Chris, who was helping her dad weed his garden, said, "I can't Brad, I'm busy." Brad continued to beg until her dad said, "Chris can't come right now, Brad, she has to help me." Brad put his hands on his hip and shouted, "I'M NOT TALKING TO YOU, TURKEY. I'M TALKING TO CHRIS!"

Brad was riding with Matt in the back seat of our Jeep Wagoneer when I got pulled over by a highway patrolman for speeding. As the trooper peered in the car, Brad started sobbing, "Are you going to take my daddy to jail?" "Well...maybe not this time, buddy," replied the smiling officer, who then whipped out his book and wrote me a ticket. I guess cute only gets you so far with the patrol.

Brad once went missing in a department store. Anne was beside herself until she saw smiling Spark walking toward her, hand in hand with the store manager. Still laughing, the manager said, "I asked him what his mom looked like. He told me, 'Oh, she's not fancy—she's just a regular mom.'"

Young Brad would often climb in bed with us in the morning because he liked to cuddle up next to the "Furnace," as he called his mom. Indeed, she was.

"I couldn't believe it!" said a mother who, at the end of a birthday party, had driven Brad and a van-load of boys across town to Baskin and Robbins for ice cream because Brad couldn't find anything he liked at the first ice cream store. After he'd heard all the flavors at Baskin and Robbins, our boy ordered… "*Vanilla!*"

"I'm going to count to three…" was a useful motivational tool in our household, particularly for Brad. On the count of "One…" Brad would continue on as if nothing had happened, perhaps even accentuating his nonchalance a bit. "Two…" might produce a giggle and a furtive glance toward the door, as suspense built. But as we puffed ourselves up for that fateful "Three!" Brad did a rapid assessment of the situation and decided to live to fight another day. He would explode out of the chair and dash through the door to perform the distasteful task, whatever it was. Fortunately, neither Anne nor I ever had to decide what happened after three.

Though the Chinese might have actually invented water drop torture, Brad certainly took it to a new level. When he started harping about something he wanted, he might keep it up for days. It failed to work most of the time, and could result in some serious time out, but Brad often felt it was worth a good-natured shot. When I told young Spencer Rose that he was almost as good at it as his Uncle Brad was, he took it as a compliment.

While in Spokane, Washington, for Expo '74, we stayed on an upper floor of the Davenport Hotel. Brad loved the ornate elevator, which he noticed lacked a 13th floor, and the plethora of elevator buttons. He pushed all of them on one long memorable trip to the lobby. Trapped with us in the car was George Gobel, a well-known comedian who was in town to perform at Expo that night. But George was a good sport; sighing, he said, "Well, folks—I guess we just took the local."

When Brad was four or five years old, he became infuriated when Matt bragged he was going to name his kids "Bruce, Michelle, Rhonda, and Lisa," using up all of the names of our neighbors' (the Rinnes) children. Brad stammered, "Well…Matt …uh…well…Matt, I'm going to name my kids Doctor Rinne and Missus Rinne!"

We lived kitty-corner from Lowell School's playground when Brad was in grade school, so we could see anyone who was playing on the school grounds. Because Brad was very social, he was usually in the middle of any physical activity he saw going on at Lowell. This was hard on his clothes, but especially hard on the glasses he wore. One of the best investments we ever made was a pair of "Battlestar Galactica" glass frames that were so rugged that they had a free replacement guarantee if broken. When we asked for a fourth replacement in one-and-a-half years, we were informed that the company had to stop making those frames.

Anne still shakes her head and shivers when she remembers looking out our upstairs bedroom window one afternoon to see seven-year-old Brad standing on the crest of the steeply gabled roof across the street, one hand on the chimney, smiling and waving at her.

Until he became too cool in middle school, Brad would repeatedly ask me to elaborate on his birth: "What did you say when I came out, Dad?" I would scrunch up my best horror face, throw my arms out wide, and scream, "EEEEEEEEAH!" Brad would roll on the floor laughing, and beg for a repeat performance.

On one of the kids' sans-parents visits to Utah, Grandpa Hansen asked Brad if he needed any money? "Oh no, Grandpa," young Brad assured him, "I've got all the money I'll ever need." When asked how much that was, he replied, "About seventeen dollars."

"How much did that cost, Dad?" was a common Brad question when we were on vacation, or at a restaurant. Because of my standard answer, he eventually began answering his own question, "Oh, let me guess—a dollar-three-ninety-eight." Then we'd both laugh, and still do.

Returning from a road trip to Oregon, we all stayed in a California 8 motel room that had a bed with a pay-per-ride vibrator. To avoid problems, Anne and I claimed that bed for the night, much to the boys' disappointment. To compromise, we gave the kids a quarter and let them try out the bed's vibrator before we all turned in. Anne and I had no sooner gotten to sleep than we were shaken awake by that miserable bed. I turned on the light to see who had dropped the quarter in the maximum vibration slot without waking us. Both kids appeared fast asleep, but Brad's grin confirmed my suspicion.

We stayed three nights at the Waldorf Astoria on a family trip to New York City. Our first morning there, we sent young Brad down to the ornate lobby to get a paper. When he returned to the room, his Mom noticed that his feet were bare. "Brad, you're supposed to wear shoes in a fancy place like this." "Don't worry Mom, I kept my feet moving so fast nobody noticed."

Brad was at his best on our family trips to Disneyland, Disney World, and Hawaii. He and Matt seemed to enjoy each other's company and were astonishingly civil to one another. But Brad once told me that his favorite family vacations were on *Skye*, our sailboat, as we explored the San Juan Islands together for four years. He said he even loved the two-week sailing vacation we took one July, when it rained almost every day. Maybe that was because he learned to beat me at checkers.

Young Brad loved the boat, being on the water, and the destination, but had some thoughts about how to improve the journey: I was at the wheel steering our full-sailing sailboat toward Lummi Island's Inati bay, when a powerboat sped by us heading in the same direction. Brad, lolling on a lazarette, said to his Mom, "Someday, I'm going to buy me a boat just like that one...." Then he looked at me and whispered to his mother: "Don't worry Mom, when I take Dad out on my boat, I'll put up a little sail to slow it down."

The Muppet Movie was Brad's favorite so he watched it over and over again on our new technological marvel, the Sony Betamax videotape machine (a losing technology in the VCR wars). Starting anywhere in the movie, Brad could quote the Muppets' lines verbatim, and still can.

Hugh Bradford's yearly Christmas classic was to take the baby Jesus from his place in our plastic crèche's manger and surreptitiously slip his neck into the crook of the shepherd's staff, causing the little acrylic infant to stick straight out horizontally. This nativity scene variant always got a laugh from visitors. Anne would scurry over and rescue the baby and place him back in the manger for the tenth time that holiday season. Young Spencer Rose, seemingly vying for Brad's family comedian position, showed me our old crèche with the poor plastic baby once again trapped in that formidable crook. He asked me, "Is this the way Brad used to do it, Gramp?"

Brad gave a lot of thought to his Christmas presents, once giving me a pair of cloth running gloves that had the individual letters of my name imprinted on the proximal fingers, "Bob" on the right and "Rose" on the left, so they could be read by anyone approaching me from the front.

As I had discovered with my mom, Brad found that the way to handle Anne was to get her laughing. But occasionally he'd forget this formula for success and would attempt to slug it out with her verbally. A famous Brad retort hurled at his mom during one heated argument was: "As soon as I'm eighteen—*you* go into a nursing home!" That did cause her to laugh, but not at that moment.

As previously mentioned, the boys got into it on occasion. Being older and stronger, Matt could pretty much have his way with Brad in an altercation, most of which were about something as earthshaking as control of the TV remote in the family room. But on one of Matt's visits home from the naval academy, he moved to show Brad his recently acquired Judo skills and found himself lifted up and pressed into the air over Brad's head. "Ah...well...OK then," he said calmly. And that was the end of all sibling combat as we knew it.

Many a parent has a story about something out of the ordinary occurring during their child's adolescence that they had no clue about at the time, but it's hard to top this one: Brad and some high school friends, collectively using the name "Buck Zane," rented a run-down basement apartment near the University, just up the road from our home on Garden Terrace. The boys each contributed five dollars toward the monthly rent, furnished the place with castoff furniture and, for a short time, used it as a place to hang out. They were eventually evicted for not paying the rent. The designated rent collector had apparently used most of the money to buy a ferret, and forgot to pay the landlord.

Brad played center on the Sehome High School football team, but his true love was rugby, the fundamentals of which he learned in Australia while on a Rotary exchange. He played that high-contact sport without glasses or contact lenses, in spite of the fact he was legally blind without them. Though he only had a blurred view of the ball's movement, teams welcomed Brad's rugby sense and power in the scrum, but they'd occasionally have to shout, "OVER HERE, BRAD!" He told me that poor vision probably helped his game because he couldn't see how big some of those guys really were.

On goose-dung-covered fields, he played first-string, slide-on-your-face (ugh!) rugby for the University of Washington. His performance there led to an invitation to play rugby in Wales for a year, after which he toured Europe. The Welsh couldn't twist their mouths around the name "Brad", but enthusiastically embraced Hugh—a Welsh name, after all. While on the tour, he and three girls he'd met were asked to tend a small hotel on Crete while the owner got a badly needed vacation. People like and trust our boy.

As he was driving to a Rolling Stones concert in Vancouver, Brad hit a deer with our little pre-owned, blue VW Rabbit. Though the windshield was smashed—in fact it had a hole in it—he and his college friends still motored to BC Place for the festivities. Can you believe no one stopped them? Coming back through the border, the guards relished his story, thought it was cool that he saw the concert anyway, and let him pass. Can you see that happening now, post 9/11?

That little blue Rabbit's engine later blew up on the freeway, so Anne took the lead in choosing his next college car, a used, white VW Rabbit that sported a "MADD" bumper sticker. The sellers, religious folks, I presume, asked Anne to pre- or post-date the check for the vehicle because they didn't think it was right to sell the car on a Sunday. We later discovered that this VW Rabbit had been previously wrecked, a fact not disclosed by those good Christians who sold it to Anne. Admittedly, a poorly matched rear body panel should have given her some pause. Not knowing the extent of the prior damage to the VW made us so nervous that we eventually bought him a brand-new brown 1991 Subaru Loyale Wagon, which later became his college graduation present.

For the sum of twenty-five dollars, I eventually sold the tired old VW to the Lummi Reservation recyclers, who swore: "We only want it for parts." Two weeks later, it was at the front of their sales lot with a four-hundred-dollar price tag on it. A month later, Anne saw the car—easily identifiable by its MADD bumper sticker, Brad's "UW" rear windshield sticker, and the off-color left rear body panel—tooling down Haxton Way, on the reservation, with four large Native Americans over-filling the front and back seats. A new bumper sticker message had been added: "F—K WAR."

Bradford lived with us for a short time after he returned from Europe, but a disagreement with his mom, something about drying his "big grungy tent" in the living room, led to his moving out, as his mother suggested, "…within 30 days!"

After Brad gave up rugby, we thought it safe to correct his vision with laser surgery. He now sees better than 20/20 in both eyes. It's great that a surgical miracle allowed us to give him something in his adulthood that we couldn't give him at birth.

After graduating from the University of Washington in industrial engineering, Brad's first job was in plastics molding at Ocean Kayaks. Then he joined Anvil Corporation, where he was introduced to the computer needs of the oil industry. Hoping to solve some of those needs, he became majority-owner of "AIS Software," a company that develops software for oil refineries, petrochemical plants, and other entities, sometimes unusual ones; one of his most intriguing early customers was an anti-technology group that asked his company to develop software that would help them put out a better newsletter.

Bonnie Warren, a lovely, smart, and talented graphic designer, was Brad's lucky break. We can thank Western Washington University and its graphic design program for luring her away from the San Francisco Bay area and Brad for having enough sense to ask her to marry him. She said yes.

The evening preceding Brad and Bonnie's summer 2006 wedding, Anne organized a terrific rehearsal dinner at the Bellingham Cruise Terminal, the Alaska Ferry's Friday departure being part of the entertainment. Guests got to take in the sights and smells of a working waterfront on that warm, late-summer evening, and the families got to know each other. Of course, we didn't tell them *everything* about ourselves. We wanted this wedding to happen.

Brad and Bonnie were married on the sunshine-bathed waterfront terrace of the Bellwether Hotel in "the finest wedding ever," according to many. As big yachts passed close by and large, multi-colored kites flew high above Zuanich park, Spencer led in Brad's dog, Lucy, and Warren helped the flower girls hurl rose petals. Then happy Brad and radiant Bonnie said their vows; Brad's Welsh friend, John, belted out an old Welsh wedding ballad; 200 guests were extremely well wined and dined; and I got to dance with my beautiful flower-girl granddaughter, Kate. Sweetface said she really liked my brand-new, dark-blue pinstripe suit that replaced my other well-worn garment, a fine, three-piece, tailor-made Hong Kong outfit that I'd purchased, in person, from "Karmani of Kowloon" fifteen years earlier. I bought a bright orange tie to impress my brother Nick, who insisted that my ties were always too drab. If you remember the polyester wardrobe story, you can see that Nick has always considered himself my fashion consultant. I guess he got that from our dad.

Bonnie is upbeat, kind, naturally artistic (first a graphic designer and now a jewelry maker), an amazing cook, and a great mother and people person. She loves Brad and has helped give his life direction. We're fortunate that Brad met Bonnie.

Augustus Robert (Gus) Rose ("Gusman") was born in the fall of 2008 at St. Joseph Hospital. His handsome face had been so well detailed on ultrasound images, we'd have recognized him anywhere. Brad immediately photographed Gus in a Washington Huskie skullcap to document that another Dawg fan had been born.

Gus loved cars (his first word) and was the only one of the grandkids who would watch the movie *Cars* with me over and over again. A "car-boat" ferry trip to Grandma and "Grandmapa's" house on Lummi Island was a big deal to little Gus.

While on the Chelan Riverwalk with the family, two-and-a-half-year-old Gus noticed that the flashing yellow crossing-walk light near the high school wasn't on, so he said to me, "Grandpa, that light needs batteries." On the same trip, I told him that our room at Campbells was the "Mothership." He said, "Grandpa, a mama ship needs a daddy ship—where's that?"

Three-year-old Gus, cuddling with Grandma on the couch, held her face between his hands and said, "Grandma, *you're* my boy." Later, after Grandma had given him a glass of orange juice, she said, "Now let's see what we can fix you for breakfast, Gus." "Oh Grandma," said Gus, "I've had all the protein I'll need for the day."

Gus once told his mother that he didn't want to go blueberry picking because, "My energy isn't right." Later, he looked at his little sister, shook his head, and said, "You know, babies can be devious."

Strapped in a car seat while passing a cemetery, Gus looked out the car window and said, "Mom and Dad—there's a statue forest."

When told he had to take Tylenol, Gus replied, with a wry smile, "...a popsicle might do the trick."

Four-year-old Gus was lying on the floor playing a board game with Tori, who was moving the pieces out of turn. I mentioned this to Gus, who was patiently trying to play with her. He philosophically observed, "She really can play the game, but she makes up her own rules."

Gus left a tap running in the bathroom, resulting in an overflow that flooded the adjacent spaces and those on the floor below. He told Grandma about it and said, "Dad was mad—*not at me*—but that it happened. I guess you don't get mad at your son unless he breaks the TV or something."

Gus and I were building with Legos when he looked up at me and said, "Grandpa, what do you think of the *afterlife*?" I was dumbfounded and proceeded to disjointedly babble a few of the philosophical things I'd learned in Mormon Sunday School before I thought to say, "Why did you ask Gus?" "Oh, I just wondered what you thought of those afterlife pyramids in Egypt. I think they're pretty cool."

While Gus was playing with a Hexbugs game, Tori came over, picked up two bugs, and started giving him her ideas. After a few minutes, Gus shook his head, took her bugs, and shouted: "WHAT ARE YOU THINKING, WOMAN?"

Gus is very bright, and has a keen spatial sense. He loves to read (finished the entire Harry Potter series at the beginning of the second grade), is building, block by block, a 3D interactive world on a video game called Minecraft, and, like his dad, is exceptionally good at Legos. Maybe he'll be the architect I almost was. I love him and am very proud of him.

Tori Anne Rose ("Torikins"), my gorgeous grandchild caboose, was born in the summer of 2011 at St. Joseph Hospital. She was a dynamo early on and seemed unflappable when Gus upended her, which was often. She loved my "Annie Mae" song, so I'm five for five on that baby-pleaser.

One-and-a-half-year-old Tori was toddling down the long hallway in our Barkley condo and was about to turn the corner, when she worriedly turned around and hurried back to Grandma Anne, murmuring, "There's a ghost!" "Oh no, Tori," said Grandma, "We don't have any ghosts in our house." Turning up her little face, those blue eyes wide, she nodded and said "…almost a ghost."

Tori pushed the small knob on our Toys"R"Us airplane and a loud jet noise was heard. Grandma said, "Oh Tori, is that an airplane noise?" "No," said Tori, shaking her head. "That's a Tori-push-a-button noise."

Two-year-old Tori had just been to the doctor for her checkup, so Grandma asked, "Did the doctor give a you shot, Tori?" "No...the doctor gave me an *appointment.*"

Tori took Anne's face in her hands and exclaimed, "Grandma, you're *sooo* precious." Later, while looking at a rainbow, she observed that, "Rainbows get stuck in my head." Still later, she said, "Sometimes my voice is very coughable, so I'll need a bottle of fizzy water."

While Cousin Kate was babysitting, Tori asked her, "How's your grandfather doing?" and then said, "Grandpa Bob is my favorite...someday I'll go to his house again."

My hose had mysteriously disappeared, so Grandma asked Tori, "Do you know what happened to Grandpa's hose?" "I think it escaped," said Tori.

When she saw a quarter moon in the middle of the day, Tori said, "Look, Grandma. The moon is already working." And when asked why she'd named her small play horse "Kitty," Tori replied," I can't help it, Grandma. That's just the way it is."

Gus was leaving with Bonnie to do a fun run at his school. I was tending Tori at the time, so I asked her, "Would you like to do a fun run, Tori?" "No, Grandpa, I'll stay at home and keep my energy in."

Tori got a timeout for crayon misuse for the umpteenth time. When she was released from confinement, she told her mom, "I don't want to live here anymore. You and Daddy are *not* nice humans."

We were tending the two kids and watching the start of a Seattle Seahawks football game a month after the Hawks had traded away one of the team's best and most explosive players. After a while, three-year-old Tori stopped helping Gus build a track for his Hexbugs, walked over to Anne seated on the couch, and shook her knee to get her attention. "Grandma, I *really* miss Percy Harvin [the traded player] but we still have Russell Wilson [quarterback] and Marshawn Lynch [running back]." Then she got back down on the floor to help Gus again.

Thanksgiving 2014 we were at the dinner table taking turns saying what we were thankful for. When it was Tori's turn, she said, "I'm thankful for the city, the moon, and the planets...I know a song about the moon...?"

Tori and Gus had a sleepover at our house on New Year's Eve of 2014. Tori slept with Grandma in the "Girl's Bunkroom," as usual. On the morning of New Year's Day, Gus and I came in to wish Grandma a happy birthday. We were all sitting on the bed talking, when Tori said, "Well, if we're going to spend all day in the same room we should decorate."

Grandma was playing a PBS *Great Performances* version of "Summertime," from *Porgy and Bess,* as Tori watched and listened attentively, fascinated by the lullaby. As the song ended, Tori remarked, "Well, she's a good singer, Grandma, but it's too loud for the baby!"

Tori told Grandma that after she ate watermelon she saved her seeds so she could plant us some watermelon trees.

Grandma said, "Tori, you're so cute." "No I'm not, Grandma, but when my hair turns white for three months in the summer, I'm adorable." And she is.

I had just taken off my sock and was examining my old deformed hammer toe. Tori watched for a while and then said, "Grandma, tell Grandpa not to feel bad about it. Every guy has one ugly toe."

At a family birthday party for Spencer, Brad was trying to light the long, multicolored candles with a grill lighter that was about out of fluid and kept sputtering out. After some good-natured ribbing by the guests, he finally gave up. Tori was quick to say, "That's OK Daddy; you tried your best."

We were tending Tori and Gus while Brad and Bonnie were at a Seahawks game in Seattle, which we were watching on TV. No surprise, it was raining heavily. Tori watched for a while and then said, "Oh Grandpa, Mommy and Daddy will get soaked...you know, *your* kid and my mommy?"

Five-year-old Tori was sitting by Grandma on one of Civic Field's grandstand benches, her first time in any stadium, watching cousin Kate run in the regional high school track and field championships. After a while, she looked up and said, "You know, Grandma, I thought these seats would be more fluffy and not so big."

"What's that little thing in the mirror, Grandma?" Tori asked pointing to our car's small compass display. "It tells me what direction I'm going, Tori," said Grandma. "Right now, it says that I'm heading north." "Grandma, my mom doesn't need one of those. She knows what direction she's going: *forward...backward...right...left.*"

Tori, Gus, and Grandma were just leaving our house with Grandma's iPad to play Pokémon Go around the condo property. Outside, I was watering the potted plants as the three gamers passed by. I said, "Well, are you guys going out to chase Pokémon?" Tori shook her head and told me, "Grandpa, *chase* is not an appropriate word for Pokémon!" Then she turned and said to Grandma, "He must have learned that in the Navy."

Tori is a joy to be around. She is very bright and is always thinking about things she has seen or heard. She never forgets a thing, and her verbal analyses are usually spot on. It looks like she will be a fine artist, like her mom. I love her and am very proud of her.

I'm proud of Brad and love him very much. He is extremely smart and practical and has a strong moral sense. He has always defended the underdog, which apparently led to quite a few fights in middle school. His sense of humor has been an enjoyable part of our lives. We thank him for Bonnie, Gus, and Tori.

A TECHNOLOGY CASCADE

In 1972, I finished diagnostic radiology training, including a neuroradiology fellowship, and joined the radiology practice in Bellingham. With me aboard, Northwest Radiologists became a four-man group serving a private office and two hospitals: St. Joseph and St. Lukes. St. Lukes eventually merged with St. Joseph as the economic realities of constantly changing and demanding technologies became apparent.

Diagnostic radiology in Bellingham was mostly general office radiology: standard X-ray films of the body, fluoroscopy of the barium-filled gastrointestinal tract, mammography, and Intravenous Pyelograms (IVP's) of the kidneys using intravenously injected contrast material ("dye" to some). At the hospitals, we did similar studies, except for mammography, and also performed the occasional crude angiogram by injecting contrast material into arteries or veins through fluoroscopically positioned catheters. Unfortunately, the makeshift sequential film sets done on the pitiful angiography equipment of either Bellingham hospital were barely readable. One had to be fearless and able to improvise. I often felt like a biplane wing walker in the early days of aviation.

The Sisters of St. Joseph of Peace eventually got tired of all the whining and cursing, and invested in a state-of-the-art cardiovascular suite that could accommodate the rapidly growing need for catheterization procedures done by radiologists and cardiologists. The sisters had one condition: I was to become a hospital-based radiologist and look after their huge investment. Worked for me!

For the first few years, my life was manageable. I could get home from the hospital at a reasonable hour, embarrass myself as *Skye's* skipper at the weekly five o-clock Bellingham Bay yacht sailing races, and expect that I'd only rarely be called back to the hospital after hours. But this was about to change as a cascade of new technology transformed the specialty.

Nuclear medicine was the first new shoe to drop as less costly and more user-friendly gamma cameras and radioactive isotope "tracers" became available. This meant that modern, state-of-the-art nuclear medicine studies could be done in the hinterlands, and that, most certainly, was us.

St. Joseph Hospital purchased the community's first gamma camera, and I soon added Director of Nuclear Medicine below the Chief of Radiology sign already on my door. Fortunately, our technologist, Debbie, had extensive training that kept us all out of trouble with the State of Washington, whose bureaucrats were extremely sensitive about how we handled and accounted for all that radioactive stuff. You'd have thought we were building a bomb.

Ultrasound technology a step up from that used for submarine hunting was the next dropping shoe. For the first time, we had a picture technique that gave us some body sectional ("slice") imaging capability. But ultrasonography was extremely operator-dependent; it required considerable skill with a hand-held transducer (sound generator/receiver) to avoid bones and gas-containing structures that could block the sound waves. Obese patients provided an added challenge and could make it a *long* day.

The practice of obstetrics and gynecology was revolutionized by the special ability of ultrasound to see through water. If a female patient drank water until her bladder was uncomfortably full, you could see the solid pelvic structures with most bowel gas pushed out of the way. Even better, the fluid-filled pregnant uterus and its enclosed fetus could now be seen with exquisite clarity. Once real-time transducers (continuous slice picture generators) became available, the fetal heart could be seen pumping, and fetal movement verified. Evaluation of fetal anatomy and measurements to determine fetal age became considerably easier.

After more crash courses, I became the Director of Ultrasound as well, but we stopped adding more signs to my door. Our super capable technologists (Carol and Nancy) and I were all learning together in the early days of ultrasound. Those two techs were by far the department's best joke tellers. They were always organizing noontime parties, and their positive attitude was infectious. Nancy's grandmother made me a little ceramic Christmas tree "…for being nice to Nancy." That little lighted tree sitting on my desk during the Christmas season always made me feel good…and still does. It's a Charlie Brown thing, I guess.

Computed Axial Tomography was then invented by the British and we had "CAT scans" (now called CT scans). I was attending the Harvard University postgraduate neuroradiology course in Boston when Hounsfield presented his first successful CT studies of the brain. They were crude images with big pixels, but we all knew that this was a game changer.

The principle of CT is simple: a narrowed x-ray beam is rotated 360 degrees around the body at the level being studied. The information is collected by detectors, spatially processed by a computer, and presented on a screen as a cross sectional slice. Advances in computer technology have allowed CT image slices to be "reconstructed" into longitudinal and oblique planes. Today, even excellent three-dimensional reconstruction is possible.

The beauty of CT is that, unlike ultrasound, x-rays are not significantly impeded by gas or bone. In fact, both are usually very helpful. Because body fat has an X-ray density all its own, the presence of fat actually makes the study easier to interpret because it separates and outlines tissues and organs. The only thing limiting the study of obese patients is the size of the hole in the CT machine they have to pass through. No matter how large they make that hole, the occasional patient is too big for it, even with pushing and squeezing. CT studies can be enhanced by intravenous contrast material, which helps the radiologist recognize blood vessels and identify body structures by their vascularity.

Even early "first generation" CT was an answer to a neuroradiologist's prayers. Prior to that, there were only four ways to get any brain information: 1) poorly to not at all by standard skull X-ray films; 2) minimally better by pneumoencephalography, during which air injected into the spinal canal is made to roughly outline the brain on radiographs, a cumbersome and painful procedure; 3) better still by nonspecific nuclear medicine imaging; and 4) considerably better by angiography, which could demonstrate blood vessel distortion and displacement. But these were indirect means of getting information. With rapid leaps in CT technology, gross anatomy and pathology of the brain could be directly and exquisitely visualized, and before long, so could that of the spine and body as well.

Magnetic Resonance Imaging (MRI) was the Brits' next quantum leap. Again, computer generated, the technology could slice image the body in any orientation by analyzing certain characteristics of magnetically excited atoms in tissue, and their change over time. This new imaging modality was most welcome when studying the brain, spine, and nervous system, where detailed anatomic images could now be obtained without radiation. Soon, other body parts, particularly the musculoskeletal structures, were also beautifully displayed.

CT and MRI became a rapidly growing part of the practice of radiology in Bellingham. Fortunately, as older associates retired, we were able to hire others to head up those programs, but we all still had to be part of the action, particularly on call, and that meant keeping many balls in the air. At my retirement party, I was handed a large jug of paper clips that I'd twisted into bizarre shapes while reading and dictating studies, and talking to physicians with the phone cradled to my ear (no speakerphone or headphone option then). Unbeknownst to me, the techs had been collecting my discarded multitasking sanity-clips for many years.

Because GE imaging equipment was considered the best at that time, we outfitted our new general radiology department, the cardiovascular suite, and, eventually, the CT and MRI labs with GE equipment (thank you, Sisters). GE's district manager, Jay Quinn, and I became good friends as he led parade after parade of curious customers through "Dr. Rose's Wonderland." Jay had six season tickets (forty-yard line) to the Seahawks games in Seattle's new Kingdome stadium, so he let our family use four of them once a year for several years. Matt and Brad got to watch legendary quarterback Jim Zorn repeatedly scramble for his life trying to complete a pass, and wide receiver Steve Largent catch those frantic passes in hall of fame fashion.

But the best head of department perk was being able to sneak the Radiology Department's closet skeleton out of the hospital each Halloween so Anne could create a scary front door tableau to greet the trick-or-treaters. The little ghosts and goblins would ask, "Is that a *real* skeleton?" We could honestly say, "You *bet* it is!" I think we even drew in revelers from Skagit County.

An aside before leaving this chapter: Carol Barnett called from the Lynden Fair, laughing. "It must be *life-size!*" she chortled, referring to a stately hospital governing board portrait of yours truly, in a pin-stripe suit, standing with my hand on the back of an expensive leather chair. I was quite the dude with my "perm'd" hair. A much smaller version of the huge photograph was already hanging on the wall leading to the hospital's cafeteria. The oversized likeness was exhibited at the County Fair and then moved to the photographer's studio window. I suppose their message was that if they can make me look good they can do it for anyone.

When the studio was finished with the big portrait they offered it to Anne for seventy-five dollars. She bought it and put it in storage, thinking that it would be bad luck to let them destroy it. I've always wondered if she'd have gone as high as a hundred bucks? The studio undoubtedly knew most people's flinch point. I've told the kids that it's OK to dump that picture after I've gone to the Happy Hunting Ground, unless someone wants it for the wall of his or her haunted house on Halloween, or for a wall hanging at a Harry Potter party—I'd love a Harry Potter party.

I retired from radiology practice in 1992. At that time, we had six radiologists covering a radiology office and all imaging and invasive procedures at St. Joseph Hospital, including a CT scanner and an MRI unit. At the time of this writing, there are 18 radiologists covering all hospital imaging and invasive procedures, and those of four outpatient imaging centers. All told, there are five MRI units, three CT scanners and a scattered host of radiology, ultrasound, and nuclear medicine devices. After decades of little change, imaging technology has made dramatic advancements, but I'm told that the practice of radiology is still a three-ring circus, clowns and all.

BELLINGHAM AND BEYOND—BITS AND PIECES

Historic Bellingham, Washington, was a bustling logging, fishing, coal producing and paper-manufacturing town in the not-too-distant past. Multi-masted schooners, barks, and steamers came and went on its large, navigable bay. Though it has morphed considerably since its robust beginnings, it still has a healthy economy, due in part to its closeness to Vancouver and Seattle. It has mild weather, very good public education, including a university, outstanding fresh and saltwater recreation, many fine parks and trails, and unrivaled mountain recreation, including skiing. In short, it's an unsurpassed town in which to live, work, rear children, and retire. And we've done all four.

Our first home was at 813 15th street on the South Hill, an older but remodeled structure overlooking the Bellingham Bay, kitty-corner from Lowell School, the oldest elementary school in the city.

Our 15th Street neighbor to the south was a retired heating-oil distributor, a widower in his eighties, who loved to take the girls from the bank for cruises on his 40-foot power-yacht. He once hired our boys to weed his garden, but we seldom saw him otherwise. On rare occasions, we could hear him playing the organ, sometimes late at night, with the lights out, which could be a little spooky.

To the north lived the Rinnes, who were very accessible and involved in our lives. They loved Brad and Matt and encouraged them to visit.

Even though Ralph Rinne was a very competent and successful surgeon in Bellingham, he and Eleanor refused to hire help of any kind. Once every year we'd see Ralph up on a long ladder leaning out and chipping off all of the old loose paint on the wood siding of their two-story home, before he touched it up. I always wondered how long it would be before he fell off the ladder, or set his house on fire with the old blowtorch he used to soften the paint, but he never did either. Weather permitting, Eleanor would hang out her wash on two big clotheslines they had strung in their back yard.

The Rinnes did all of their own lawn care and gardening and some of ours in the abutting flowerbeds between our two homes. One winter, Ralph severely cut back a large old forsythia bush that faced the street on our property line. He assured me, "Don't worry, Bob, you just can't kill those things!" Well, next spring we found out that, against all odds, the patient had indeed died. Ralph was embarrassed, to say the least. But before I could file a malpractice suit, he dug up the body, hauled in a few bags of topsoil, and planted the largest nursery-propagated flowering forsythia bush I had ever seen. I'll bet he wished that his extremely rare surgical complications could have been so easily fixed.

Across the street and downhill toward the water lived the Roches. She was a professor at the university, a private person whom we rarely saw. But then there was John, an unusual neighbor to say the least. A Harvard-trained surgeon, I was told. Amazing fact.

Always looking for a great deal, John bought a few tons of chicken manure through the classifieds. There was a lot of liquid in that huge dumped truckload, so, lava-like, it began sliding downhill toward the bay. The brindle-brown odoriferous mass even crept across an alley before stopping in the Olivers' yard below. The prevailing wind reminded us of John for weeks.

While shaving, John leaned back against a wall of his bathroom and it promptly gave way, causing him to fall on his back in his admittedly fine organic vegetable garden. Though I had some doubts about John, his diagnosis of carpenter ants was right on. To discover the extent of the infestation, he took up a chain saw and, with true surgical flare, made large holes in most of the remaining walls of the bathroom. While he was at it, he cut away all but the major supports to a living room wall that fronted the grade school across the street—"to get a view". After covering these self-inflicted wounds with clear plastic sheeting, he spent the rest of the summer, and most of the fall, trying to find a human carpenter to repair the damage.

On a warm summer night, Anne and I were getting ready for bed when I heard a shriek: *"BOB, THE WINDOW."* Creeping over the sill of the raised bedroom window facing the bay was the largest bat I have ever seen. As it began to flutter about the room, I shouted, "Get under the covers—I'll be back!" I rushed from the room, slammed the door, ran down the stairs to the basement, put on my wetsuit, helmet, and gloves, grabbed a large fishnet, and ran backwards (because of the flippers) back upstairs. I heard a muffled undercover whimper: *"Bob...where are you?"*

Using the fishnet as a shield, I removed my lovely lady from her hiding place, escorted her out of the room, returned, closed the door, put the net in front of my face, snagged the darting creature out of mid-air and pinned it to the bed. Momentarily immobilized was the gnashing-toothed face of the meanest looking little critter I'd ever seen. I carefully scooped the menace up into the net, carried it to the window, shook it free and watched it dart away into the moonlit night. After removing my wetsuit helmet, I placed it on my arm like a knight of old before swaggering downstairs, sans flippers, to receive m' lady's accolade: "Bob, what took you so long?"

The next weekend, we had just moored our sailboat in Roach Harbor when a person we barely knew from the sailboat races said, "I hear you had a bat in your bedroom."

Bellis Fair mall opened in 1988 and immediately sucked most of the men's stores out of downtown Bellingham. But the House of Provius, staffed by two unique owner-salesmen, survived and prospered. On my half day off I'd often stop by there to discuss the latest fashions—Bellingham's own version, that is—with George and Harold. The dialogue was predictable:

George: (small, thin, swarthy, well dressed, of Greek descent) "Hey, Doc, how're yah doin'? Just wait till you see the new coats we got in. I even bought one for myself. They've been just flying off the rack, haven't they, Harold?"

Harold: (watchmaker type face, wire rimmed glasses low on his nose) "Sure have, George."

George: "Doc, just try one on. You won't be sorry [pause in conversation while I put the on the coat]. Ohhh, it looks *great!* Don't you think, Harold?"

Harold: "Looks good to me, George."

Doc: "Oh, I don't know, George—I, uhhh [shaking head while looking in mirror]."

George: "Hey, Doc, take it home and show it to Rose."

Harold: "Yeah, take 'it home. I think she'll like it."

Doc: "OK, I'll show it to *Anne.*"

George: "You won't be sorry, Doc. Be sure to say hello to Rose." (Exit Doc with plaid coat. You might guess what "Rose" thought.)

Shopping in the House of Provius was good relaxation. But if Anne did like something, there was always the risk that we'd see it again in Bellingham's relatively small men's fashion scene. Bill Winter and I showed up at a medical society dance in identical tan polyester leisure suits. We agreed that we were probably the two grandest tigers in *that* jungle, a nebulous distinction.

Campbells Resort on Lake Chelan became the yearly family vacation spot in 1972. For that first year, we rented a no frills cabin with kitchen facilities. Our miniature dachshund, Skippy, accompanied us, but that was a move we'd soon regret. As if in a National Lampoon movie, old Skip promptly disappeared into the crawl space beneath the conjoined cabins, where he began noisily chasing little animals, an activity for which his breed was created. We'd occasionally lure him out, but eventually he'd manage to escape our grasp and scoot back into the space, barking incessantly. Because of the withering stares of the other cabin guests, we realized that our neighbors weren't amused by old Skip, so he spent the remainder of his vacation time as a houseguest of Chelan's veterinarian.

The following year we moved our dog and pony show to room 2112, in a larger building fronting the lake, the "Mothership," as it became affectionately known. Not surprisingly, we saw NO PETS ALLOWED signs when we arrived for that second Campbells vacation, but that was OK because we'd already made other arrangements for Skippy, so technically, our show was sans pony and sans dog. Be that as it may, except for 1994, when the hotel staff warned us off because the nearby Tyee forest fire was contaminating the air and water, the Rose family has managed to bring some type of summer act to Chelan, yearly.

Matt and Brad's Campbells routine was predictable: run with Dad in the morning, devour fancy Pershings at Judy-Jane's bakery, dive in the lake, get warm in the hot tub, swim in the pool, jump off the high dive, swim across the lake to the Caravel, jump off the bridge when the Sherriff wasn't looking, and play water volleyball. After lunch, which might include a lunchtime sail across the lake for hamburgers, the morning water routine would resume. Sunbathing, books, and looking at girls occupied their downtime, punctuated by the occasional short walk into town, where they might run into Mom at Manning Drugs or Clampits Chelan Fashions. Rare rainy days might include a family trip to a Columbia River dam or a movie.

At day's end, they would often skip dinner at Campbells so they could walk to the drive-in by themselves, ride the Go-carts, and play miniature golf. But what the boys liked best was spending the night outside on the "point" in sleeping bags, if they chose to, and they usually did. This was our kids' first exposure to small-town life and they loved it (as do their progeny—"better than Christmas!").

Anne and I experienced a unique European adventure in 1975, when we flew into Frankfurt, Germany, to join Jane and John Coons on a road trip. Because John was an army dentist in Crailsheim, we could stay in unbelievably inexpensive (sometimes as low as six dollars a night per couple, per room) Armed Forces Recreation Center lodgings in Germany and France. The finest of these were the Champs-Elysees Hotel (just off the famous boulevard) in Paris, and the General Walker Hotel (formerly the Third Reich hotel Platterhoff, where Hitler wrote *Mein Kampf*) in the SS enclave of Obersalsberg, above Berchtesgaden in Bavaria. From the Paris lodging we made a game effort to take in the City of Light in two days. With Uncle John leading the charge, we got up early and didn't miss much.

The General Walker was close to the mouth of a tunnel dug deep into a mountain, from which a polished brass elevator ascended to Hitler's Eagle's Nest retreat perched high above Berchtesgaden. The idyllic *Sound of Music* view of green meadows and snow-capped Alps that could be seen from the nest was truly astonishing. It's good old Adolph didn't live to enjoy it.

It's not the destination, it's the journey…right? That was certainly true touring Europe in John's old Chrysler sedan. Riding shotgun, it was my job to lean out the window and manually work the mechanically linked windshield wipers when it rained. John somehow twice talked himself through the tight German/French border in spite of the broken wipers and the car's bald tires—unheard of. I'm telling you, those Germans looked and acted like the border guards in a World War II movie. As we drove away, we all looked straight ahead. I kept waiting for the dreaded shout, *"HALT!"* followed by the inevitable submachine gun fire.

Once in France, I suggested that we might try one of the roadside restaurants, which we'd heard were very good, but John, Paris-bound, had brought a big bowl of radishes, so we ate those. Even John eventually got tired, so we pulled off the road and drove down a short lane to a chain-link fence, where we parked in the dark, hoping that we could all take a nap. We were suddenly jolted wide-awake as the world around us exploded—shock and awe, as it were. The fence signs, which none of us could read, must have said "Warning—Artillery Firing Range," or something like that. We'd apparently parked in the middle of a nighttime French army war exercise.

We began sailing in the mid-1970s. Anne and I crewed on a large sailboat that was competing in the weekly Bellingham Bay yacht races. We had so much fun we bought a new Cal 2-29, a twenty-nine-foot cruiser/racer that sported a navy-blue hull, white deck and trim, a white steering wheel, and too much teak for my taste. We named it *Skye*, after the Scottish isle. To save money, we outfitted the shiny new boat ourselves.

Our shakedown cruise was memorable. Anne, our two untrained boys, and I were the only crew on Skye's first weekend family trip to Cyprus island. Returning home, we were blithely flying the big spinnaker approaching Bellingham bay, when a south wind suddenly picked up behind us and the boat began surfing in large waves. We performed a disorganized spinnaker takedown, which resulted in an unplanned over-the-side sail-washing, but we somehow managed to get the big sail in. Unfortunately, the boat was still hurtling toward the harbor breakwater with the wind behind us and the mainsail and Jenny still up. I sent the boys below, where they laughed and shouted about how much fun this was...*uh-huh*. Then, we headed up into the wind so we could lower the two big sails. Anne got the Jenny in and below without too much difficulty, but as she rapidly lowered the mainsail, the boom and attached mainsail crashed down on my head. When my mind cleared, I made a mental note to move a topping lift installation, which would have prevented the mishap, to the top of my to-do list. Of course, that would require my being winched to top of the mast, a trip I'd obviously been avoiding.

Fortunately, our boat's little one-lung diesel engine—which should have been started before we began all of this—chugged to life, and we motored into the harbor with our mainsail still embarrassingly draped over the deck and cockpit for all to see.

After that Cyprus outing, I thought I might be sailing solo in the future, but by the next weekend everyone was game to go again. That was good news because Anne knew as much about sailing as I did and was indispensable. So the Rose crew headed out for a long weekend at Sucia Island, and had a great time. It was while we were anchored in Sucia's Shallow Bay that we saw a sailboat from Seattle motor in and tie up to the loop of line protruding from a crab pot float. I said to Anne, "Do we tell 'em?" We did. They promptly motored out, purposely avoiding eye contact, which was difficult because they had to go close abeam to get around us.

We had a similar experience while we were anchored in Lummi Island's Inati Bay. An incoming Cal 2-29, just like ours, but white, sailed past the breakwater and did a one-eighty as it reached our starboard beam. It momentarily stopped and the boat's anchor was tossed overboard. But in spite of the full reverse propulsion, which was churning up the water, the boat began moving slowly forward. We heard the captain shout, "There must be a strong current, the anchor's dragging!" We all sat there incredulous—the sails were still up and set. Do we tell 'em? This time we didn't; we just watched. After a flurry of activity, they retrieved that dragging anchor and sailed out of the bay, barely missing Inati's rocky entrance shoal as they departed. We all wondered if they ever figured it out?

We were usually lucky with weather, until we decided to take a two-week sailing vacation in June. The first two days spent in San Juan Island's Garrison Bay were warm and beautiful. We dug clams, had our catch checked by a large-busted female Fish and Wildlife "Ranger" dressed *only* in bib overalls (to Matt and Brad's delight), and checked out the Pig War artifacts ashore. But after this great start, the weather turned lousy, which precluded our exploring the Gulf Islands to the north as we had planned. Instead, for two or three days at a time, we'd check out easy-to-motor-to anchorages in the San Juan Islands and then motor to the dock in Friday Harbor, where we could take a welcome shower, grab some spaghetti at the only restaurant in town, and go to a movie. We repeated this pattern until it was time to go home. Unfortunately, the movie never changed, so the boys soon memorized the dialogue and periodically whispered the anticipated lines, always good for a laugh. While at anchor in various bays, we rowed ashore and explored, read, told stories, and played checkers or chess. In the words of Martha Stewart, "It was a good thing."

During the above-mentioned Garrison Bay two-day-calm, our miniature dachshund, Skippy, swam back and forth to the beach from our anchored boat, accompanying any crew member who went ashore. All you could see was the wake of his little nose moving through the water like a snorkel. We watched him closely and, with the help of the dinghy, hauled him aboard whenever he returned to the boat. But on one occasion, he swam too close to a large yacht and its skipper jumped in to save him—*how embarrassing!* Sitting like a potentate in the bow of the Good Samaritan's dingy, old Skip was returned to us. We thanked the dripping-wet rescuer profusely and confined Skippy to his quarters below, until the big yacht motored out. Then we let old Skip resume his supervised exercises.

Contrary to our experience with Skippy in Chelan, he was great on our family boat trips. He'd sit up on one of the lazarettes, sniffing the air, seeming to pay closer attention to what was going on than most of the crew.

Skippy often jumped from the boat while we were anchored, but his leap into Hales Pass while we were under sail was almost his last. This impromptu act prompted our first man-overboard (this-is-not-a) drill, the results of which made us realize that we had to rethink our rescue procedures. With Anne holding my legs, I tried unsuccessfully to scoop up the snorkeling Skipper as he passed beneath the stern of the boat. In desperation, I snagged his collar with a boathook and hoisted the choking and sputtering dog aboard. At that point, I think old Skip came to grips with the ineptness of the crew, because he became decidedly more careful. But we kept a salmon net handy, just in case. The young humans on board sometimes showed even less judgment than Skippy, so I bought a swim ladder for them.

More cruiser than racer was our "cruiser-racer" sailboat. That could probably be said for the captain as well. We couldn't point as high into the wind as I would have liked, and we had a steering wheel instead of a tiller. I was told that "lessened the feel," whatever that was. But our good-natured crew had a great time racing on Bellingham Bay. We only won a time or two over our four years of racing, usually thanks to some fluke wind shift the other boats didn't get.

We all enjoyed the competitive camaraderie of Bellingham's sailing community, especially the jocular post-race buffets at the yacht club. It was at one of those jovial events that someone brought a blowup plastic woman, bought at an adult bookstore, and passed it around the dining tables for inspection. Even the non-inflatable women thought that was interesting.

During four years of sailing and motoring *Skye*, we saw most of the San Juan Islands and, on many, did some exploring ashore. We were captivated by the hermit of Matia ruins, delighted by Roach Harbor's cannon at sundown, and spellbound by the phosphorescent organisms that sometimes dripped from our oars as we rowed about our anchored boat at night. To every one's delight, these light-emitting creatures could also be seen rushing through the bowl of our boat's seawater-flushing toilet, causing all of us to give it a few extra pumps at night. We were often surprised by the power of the elements and how quickly things could change. But mostly, we remember the breath-taking beauty and the myriad sounds and smells of the San Juan archipelago, a special place.

When we sold *Skye*, we bought a second-hand, trailerable International 420 dinghy, a high-performance centerboard sailboat. I could never get that boat to sail really well, in part because none of my crew would hang out on the boat's aging trapeze the way those Olympians did...at least that's my analysis. Sure, we'd sail across Lake Chelan to get hamburgers, which gave us a purpose, but after we'd eaten those burgers, all we could think about was getting back to Campbells so we didn't miss anything. If there wasn't wind, we'd use a paddle.

At Silver Lake, the old daysailer became a fish-trolling platform from which we'd try to catch a few small state-planted trout for supper. Talk about Silver Lake and I smell the fragrant fir and cedar trees, taste Anne's Coleman stove breakfasts and lantern-lit suppers, and feel the good but sometimes itchy swimming (thanks to those little cercaria we forgot to wash off). I also miss smoky, marshmallow-roasting campfires we'd all sing around before we climbed into those cozy sleeping bags, scattered about the floor of that huge striped-roof family circus tent we'd all put up in the dark...*the best!*

Windsurfers replaced the 420 sailboat. Though Matt got fairly good at windsurfing, my skills could be best described as a work in progress, despite the fact that Arlen Burns and I practiced windsurfing on Lake Samish and Bellingham Bay each summer, Arlen on a crude fiberglass board he'd made himself. My craft was store-bought and should have been easier to deal with, but at the beginning of every summer, I felt like I was unsteadily hoisting up and trying to handle that big windsurfer sail for the first time.

Without a powerboat of our own, we rarely went salmon fishing. So when Dave Jones asked Matt, Brad, and me to accompany his son and him on a one-day fishing trip we were more than delighted. Dave had patiently, and sometimes at great personal risk, learned how to fish Puget Sound from an eccentric, borderline psychotic, mutual acquaintance of ours, who occasionally flipped out (reportedly killing his ex-wife's lover by excising his manhood), but always got fish.

After a morning of fishing, we'd caught a few Silver salmon, well within our collective limits in those days, and were preparing to head home because Dr. Dave was on call that evening. But on an impulse, Captain Dave decided that we should make a run at the kelp beds off the east side of Saturna Island. On our first pass, we hooked a forty-pound King salmon that dove to the bottom, fighting us hard for forty-five minutes before tiring enough that we could net it. After an equally hard and time-consuming second-pass battle, we caught that first Chinook's forty-one-pound schoolmate, which prompted the young crew to beg the skipper for another run through the kelp. "Sorry guys," said Dave, "but I really better get back." So we left the kelp beds and headed home, ending a once-in-a-lifetime experience for us all—including Cap'n Dave, as it's turned out.

In 1981, we bought a three-level, bay-view house, built on the hillside near Western Washington University. Brad was furious with us for moving him away from the Lowell School action, but we needed a larger home for our soon-to-be teenagers. They immediately spread out over the lower of two living levels, counting as theirs the big family room that was soon to be remodeled. The lowest floor, snuggled over the rocky hillside, was a large woodworking shop that I miss to this day. Every floor of our new home had a door to the outside, a mixed blessing with teenagers (remember Brad and the Buck Zane club just up the street?).

We'd no sooner settled in at Garden Terrace than Anne became interested in politics, starting as a community activist in Eco-Action, a group of women trying to preserve Bellingham's waterfront for parks and trails. Rather than tie themselves to trees like many environmental activists did in those days, they convinced the Rotary Club that it should gather forces to acquire the land that is now Boulevard Waterfront Park and give it to the city. Later, while she was serving two terms on the Bellingham City Council, five years as its president, she was able to see that Boulevard Park was actually funded and built on its valuable Bellingham Bay waterfront property. Her misspelled name is cast on a nice little bronze plaque, somewhere in the park.

The kids and I were proud of her community service, but those city council meetings were hard to sit through. I did enjoy doorbelling for her, when she was campaigning, and I was a pretty good campaign sign putter-upper.

After two years of weekend and some nighttime commutes to Seattle for classes, Anne got her Executive MBA from the University of Washington. Her organizational skills were such that our routine seemed hardly interrupted. This degree was useful when she was appointed to the State Housing Finance Commission, which had just been formed to help provide funding for low-income housing. Suddenly, Anne was flying all over the state and country for meetings, but I maintained that there'd never been a meeting Anne didn't like.

Our move to Garden Terrace was Skippy's downfall. On his second space-walk from our 30-foot high upper deck—lucky the first time, I guess—old Skip slipped some disks and had to be put to sleep. We loved that fearless little dog who would take on a German Shepard if he thought it needed doing. It's for sure that no mailman or paperboy could sneak up on us while Skippy was alive.

We tried to replace old Skip with a Pomeranian pup that Anne found at a pet store. I can still remember her bringing him to the hospital's parking lot to show me: "Bob...he's sooo cute!" "Anne, have you ever seen an ugly pup?"

Teddy grew into a larger-than-breed-sized, Pomeranian-like, hyperactive diarrhea machine that could literally jump three feet in the air. He trashed the lower living level, where we tried, without much luck, to contain him. After he'd chewed up most of the baseboards and anything with legs, including people, we decided that we had to take Teddy back to the pet store and beg them to them to keep him. Then an incredible stroke of luck: a woman saw Anne carrying the soon-to-be-returned Teddy through the pet store parking lot, thought he was "sooo cute," and bought him on the spot for twenty-five dollars. We prayed that she hadn't copied down Anne's license plate number. Each ring of the telephone caused us considerable anxiety for the next few days.

Teddy's damage to the lower living level hurried a remodel of the family room and kitchen by our neighbor, Gordon Nichols, a retired shop teacher and meticulous craftsman. The piece de resistance of the project was a new oak-trimmed gas fireplace in the family room. As a family project, Anne had the kids glue four thousand pennies to the large horizontal copper surface of the elevated hearth. A few valuable coins were scattered among the others so that the kids had something to hunt for with their friends.

To make the family room more teenager friendly, we added a three-fourths size oak pool table, a big-screen front-projected TV set, and a very expensive Sony Betamax video tape recorder, a fine but doomed technology in the ensuing video tape recorder wars. We knew how to pick a winner.

Soon after we'd moved into the newly remodeled kitchen, we had a party. Anne had just removed the protective wire from the top of a bottle of champagne and was talking to someone as her warm hand lingered on the cold bottle's neck. Suddenly, the cork exploded out of the bottle and drilled a hole in the overhead light diffuser, barely missing her eyes. She always insists that it was I that who was holding the bottle, but I'm telling the story and I'm not about to admit to poor judgement like that.

Large skylights we'd put in the kitchen we're a mixed blessing; though we could now better see the sky and trees in the daytime, at night we'd often get the feeling that we were being watched. We'd look up to see many little eyes staring down at us, a few bored raccoons who'd decided to see what the Roses were doing. This was usually after they'd gorged themselves on dog food that a pair of our college professor neighbors had put out for them in a kid's plastic swimming pool. When the raccoons weren't dining, the rats were.

The next Christmas, Santa cured our post Skippy grief with a pick of the litter Balinese kitten. Having found tickets to the "Otis Express" in our Christmas stockings, we hurriedly climbed aboard the old decorated Wagoneer and drove to the kitten-keepers so we could pick out our new pet. Just like little Skippy, Otis padded right to up to the boys and became an instant family member.

Not at all skittish, Otis loved people and considered himself one of the guys. Unusual for a cat, he wanted to be where the action was. He was extremely smart and would cat-talk to us about a lot of things. He understood an unbelievable number of our words and would respond appropriately to those that affected him. He would always come promptly when called. How many cats do you know that will do that?

Otis knew when the boys should arrive home from school and was at the door waiting for them. If they were late, he'd loudly let them know how distressed he was. Then he'd groan with pleasure as they picked him up; he liked to be cradled. Otis slept near the head of the bed with Matt and Brad. He especially liked the warmth of Matt's waterbed. When the boys' alarms went off, or we called them, he'd harshly meow in their faces, scolding them like a drill sergeant until they got up or answered us.

Otis and the boys had a game they loved to play; he'd hide on the top living room level and one of the boys would creep up the stairs to find him. When they peered up over the floor edge, Otis would suddenly swoop over and box their head with both paws before running off to hide again. The kids said that it was a bit nerve-wracking because they never knew what direction he'd come from, and he was so fast that they couldn't react before he counted coup like a Lakota Sioux warrior.

After Matt and Brad moved out, Otis decided that he'd sleep with Anne and me. The first night he tried to curl up near our heads, as he had with boys. I got up, grabbed a towel, put it at the bottom of the bed between Anne and me, placed the cat on it, and said, "Otis, you sleep there!" He did thereafter, without fail. But just as he had done with the kids, when the alarm went off, Sergeant Otis was up sounding reveille in my face.

In 1983, a friend notified us that a "For Sale" sign had just appeared in front of a cabin near hers on the north side of Lummi Island's Lane Spit. The seller, from Oregon, had inherited his father's two-bedroom home and was tired of trying to manage it as a rental. Fortunate for us, they'd listed with an elderly island realtor who, within the week, was planning to leave on a one-month vacation in Europe, so he was aching to make a quick, unencumbered sale. Old Ted knew that homes on this low-bank sandy beach were in high demand, seldom turned over, and often sold by word of mouth, so he hoped to sell it before some other realtor got a crack at it. He hadn't even advertised it in the Bellingham Herald. We couldn't afford the asking price but we came up with a low-ball offer, thinking he'd probably laugh at us. Ted quickly countered, "Put another $5,000 with that and I'll tell them that it's the best deal they can hope for in the present market."

After we gave it an outside coat of paint, and built a large treated-wood deck facing the water, we had a deal-of-a-lifetime island retreat. Ted, by the way, had one fine, worry-free vacation.

We soon suspected, and the neighbors confirmed, that the cabin's eighty-year-old former owner had been a ladies' man. The back bedroom had apparently been inhabited by a parade of girlfriends, who, in turn, had enjoyed the room's private outside entrance, adjoining half bath, and kitchen facilities that included a pink stove and pink refrigerator. But Otto was totally in control of the house action; the only door lock between the two living spaces was on his side.

Otto had obviously cut some cost corners while building some parts of the cabin, an obvious example being an electric light cord, fastened to the wall by staples, which substituted for wiring in a crudely walled-off television roomlet. Anne was bemoaning this one-day so, to make her feel better, I reminded her that the roof was almost new. "We won't have to worry about that anytime soon," I assured her. The very next January a neighbor called to report that a Northeaster the previous night had blown off all our roofing, which was now a scattered and crumpled heap on the lawn between our cabin and the street. A roofer who came out in sub-freezing temperatures to help me cover the remains, awaiting roof replacement, said that he had never before seen so few nails and plies of material used. "Must have been one hell of a deal," he mumbled.

The roof notwithstanding, we had some great times in that old pre-remodel cabin. Windsurfing was big for a while. I fell in a lot, but clambered out fast because, even with a wetsuit on, that water was *cold*. A shift to kayaks even involved Anne. She and I took lessons and we both learned to Eskimo Roll, believe it or not, but we mutually vowed that we'd never make that necessary. "Stay together…near the shore" was the mantra we took away from kayak school.

Though the inter-tidal portion of our accretion beach was an ever-changing balance of sand and gravel, the beach above the high tide line was mostly gravel when we first moved there. But Mother Nature eventually intervened with three days of strong westerly winds, and the beach was miraculously and permanently transformed into Hawaii-like sand ten inches deep. God preparing for the grandkids, I guess.

One bright summer morning, Gene Long, our neighbor across the street, ran up and down the beach shouting, "It's a herring ball—it's a herring ball!" The entire bay was a speckled sea of white and grey as thousands of birds, mostly gulls, frantically darted about, thrashing the water, gobbling down countless small fish they'd plucked from an enormous school of herring. This frenetic activity went on for hours. Sure enough, at very low tide we could see thick sleeves of herring eggs covering the eelgrass, a great thing for future salmon. Unfortunately, for whatever reason, that was a one-time happening in our bay.

"We see seals...so there *must* be salmon" was a common saying at the Spit. This was certainly true for the first two weeks of September, 1993, when, accompanying the sighting of an unusually large number of our four-flippered friends, we shore dwellers began catching five-to-seven-pound Silver Salmon from our beach almost every evening. We soon discovered that the fish went for Krocodile lures almost exclusively, so we raced each other to town, and to neighboring cities, to buy up all the Krocs we could find. The eelgrass was snagging a lot of our lures, and we all knew that we might never get this chance again.

The oracles of the beach postulated that, due to a fairly dry summer, this run of Silvers was just milling around out there waiting for rain to increase the water flow in native streams so that the fish could smell their way home. Sure enough, after a big rainstorm they were gone. I caught my last Coho of that run in that downpour. It seemed a larger specimen than we'd been catching—and me with no fish scale to weigh it. Fish in hand, I ran up and down the beach trying to find someone with a scale. Fortunately, a neighbor came to my rescue with a scale and a camera. She weighed and photographed my eleven-pound two-ounce beauty (a size usually only caught in the ocean) and, after I'd long forgotten about it, sent me a witnessed photo of the rare event with her Christmas card.

So how did our cat like the beach? Otis loved all of those new smells, critters, and treats, but he hated the car ride out there. He would occasionally escape his box and jump onto the dashboard, or my lap, all the while emitting a loud guttural noise of fear and protest. But once at the beach, he would patrol the neighborhood, sometimes depositing a seemingly dead snake in the house when he returned home. Otis would soon get bored and leave the snake free to hide under the couch and slither out when the coast seemed clear. The most memorable slither was between Carol Barnett's feet at a party we were giving. Carol jumped off the couch screaming as the snake rapidly slithered toward the open door.

Our super-cat had been gone for a long time, one afternoon, when Matt heard him meowing loudly and saw him sitting on the beachside windowsill of our elderly next-door neighbor's house. Otis wouldn't come when called, which was unusual for him. When Matt walked over to get the cat, he could see Mable lying on the living room floor, apparently in distress. She had broken her hip and had apparently been lying there moaning for quite some time. Otis had probably saved her life.

RETIRED BOB

Debilitating atrial fibrillation was one of the reasons I retired in 1992, that and the fact that both of my parents had died at age fifty-nine, of heart related issues. After unsuccessfully trying to control my AF with drugs—some potentially more dangerous than the rhythm disorder—my cardiologist confided, "Many of my fibrillation patients just take Coumadin (to prevent stroke) and digitalis (to control heart rate), exercise, and learn to live with their fibrillation. They do pretty well." So I took my meds, ran daily, did my best to ignore the symptoms, and eventually did pretty well. During an office visit, I told my doc that his advice had worked. "Did I really say that? And it worked? Well, what do you know!"

Retirement gave us an opportunity to find out more about our inner selves as we began taking courses in Ericksonian Hypnosis, encouraged by Dr. Charles Kerber, an old friend and neuroradiology mentor. Chuck used hypnosis to control pain in his angiography patients and had taught Anne self-hypnotic techniques that helped her deal with her migraines. Drs. Yapko, Zeig, and others, helped us learn the many induction and patient management techniques that define the specialty. Ericksonians believe that anyone can be hypnotized and treated, if managed properly. In the learning process, we had many fascinating trance experiences and became pretty darn good hypnotists, both receiving our Ericksonian Hypnotherapy certifications. Of course, we also both became trance junkies and had to enter a ten-step program to kick the habit.

Our friend, Chuck Kerber MD, was a master showman as well as a top-notch neuroradiologist. Because he knew I was a good hypnosis subject, he suggested that we have a little fun one afternoon. After getting my permission for the procedure—important in Ericksonian trancework—he put me in a deep awake trance and, while I watched, stuck a large gauge needle through the middle of a big vein he'd been eyeing on the back of my hand. He immediately pulled the needle out, producing copious bleeding from the needle holes on either side of the vein. Then he suggested that the bleeding should stop, which it promptly did, and start again, which was no problem with those big needle holes. But that wasn't enough for Chuck, the performer. He suggested that holes on either side of the vein should stop bleeding individually, first medially and then laterally, and they did. Does that cure any doubts you might have had about there being a mind-body connection? With all the possibilities of the discipline, it's unfortunate that hypnosis is such a fertile ground for quackery, but it has been for ages.

Soon after I retired, both of our adjoining neighbors' septic systems failed. A retirement present I guess. Because of this, we thought it prudent to drill a deep well for drinking water, add a chlorinator for safety, and use the shallow old groundwater well for irrigation only. Just before drilling, Gene Long volunteered his services as a water witch. Using bent metal welding rods in each hand as sensing sticks, he soon mapped out an underground stream of water on the southwest side of the property, the rod tips indicating water presence by spontaneously converging. Sure enough, sixty feet down, we hit water flowing at six to eight gallons per minute. Because all other wells on the spit have had to be drilled down two hundred feet or more to find water, we've always credited Gene for our good fortune.

That water witch exercise was spooky. We determined that Anne also had the witching-gift (no pun intended), but no matter how hard I tried, I couldn't get those sticks to do anything. However, if Gene vigorously rubbed his palms on mine, even I could make the rods work for a minute or so. Don't ask me why. Those metal sticks just seemed to have a life of their own and would not be denied.

We remodeled the cabin in 1992, so we could eventually live there full-time. We'd hoped to just add four hundred square feet of bathroom, pantry, laundry, and kitchen space, but it soon became apparent that the whole house needed a major do-over. So we added a utility room, where an old gravel-floored garage had been, and brought the insulation, plumbing, and electrical up to code. Unfortunately, that meant Otto's old TV-plug-in light cord had to go. The finished home cost three times the initial estimate (it's only money, right?), but the funky old cabin was indeed transformed.

A sturdy new propane-burning Honda generator became our security blanket against those awesome Northeasters and their six-to-eight-foot waves, which crashed ashore, chopping and washing away our inter-tidal sandy beach two to three feet down. Beach mud and salt soon cloaked our windows during those blows, and it seemed like we were living in a cave, eagerly awaiting a temperature rise to above freezing so we could safely hose off our double pane glass windows. At least we had heat, light, refrigeration, a microwave, and a TV, while we waited two or three days for the wind to die down and the power to come back on. The chopped-away beach would slowly accrete back to its previous state, sometimes surreptitiously helped along by a friend's little Bearcat bulldozer. Agate hunting was at its best after a Northeaster. One good thing, I guess.

In 1999, we sold our South Hill home and moved to the beach permanently. Though we loaned or gave most of the contents of that big house to Matt, Brad, Goodwill, or the garbage dump, boxes containing family history books, pictures, stuffed bears, bagpipes, woodworking tools, and other detritus of then thirty-five years of marriage ended up in the constant sixty-degree darkness of three big, heated storage units. Several family happenings later, we have worked the residual down to a stack along a bedroom wall in Brad and Bonnie's basement. I'm going to designate Brad as the family historian and beg him to keep it.

About the bagpipes mentioned and our Scottishness: we got caught up in our Scotch heritage soon after we first moved to Bellingham, in 1966. With the encouragement and tutoring of a piper friend, John Munroe, I began working hard on practice chanter grace notes and trills. Because I seemed to show some promise, Anne presented me with a fine set of Scottish bagpipes and I was soon attacking the frustrating art with a sometimes-dissonant fervor, hugging the Bellingham pipe band edges, so to speak. We were often invited into *other* Scottish homes to hear competitive pipers from the U.S. and Canada blare and wail away so they could be good naturedly critiqued by their peers, an entertaining tradition hundreds of years old. For a time, the Highland Games became the highlight of the year, even after my amateur pipe playing slacked off, and then stopped altogether. Aye...I surrendered my pipe-band-kilt and sporran, sad to say.

But retirement allowed me to fulfill this Scottish clansman's dream: Anne and I made a pilgrimage to the Rose Clan homeland near Inverness, Scotland, on one of its few sunny days. We celebrated this good fortune with a special Scots dinner, complete with haggis, followed by a performance featuring the Royal Scottish Philharmonic Orchestra, both held in the city's new modern concert hall. This gala only happens in Inverness one Sunday a year and was all sold out, except for two front row tickets, which they let us have. Fortuitous timing. Fortunately, Anne had suggested that we dress up, rather than wear our usual Bellingham event fashion attire, which was good, because most of those Scots were turned out in suits and fancy dresses. But my tweed sport coat and Rose tartan tie at least showed an effort, and seemed acceptable.

After the concert, we stayed overnight at close-by Kilravock castle, built in 1460, where exposure to Rose clan lore stirred our souls. Early the next morning, with wisps of fog still rising from the moors, we tromped Culloden's historic battlefield, all the while cursing the British for their brutality to, and massacre of, our brave ancestors.

So why did we need a costly Y-DNA study to prove that we Roses were Scottish (a certainty, to me) rather than English or Dutch? We Scots are frugal, you know. But to be good sports, we ponied up our contribution to the effort and soon forgot about it. Then Kathleen Rose, our well-meaning family genealogist, shot an arrow through my heart when she called to report: *"We're not Scottish—we're Dutch!"* I was slow to heal from that missile. No more were the massed pipe bands as rousing, the tumbling caber as exhilarating, or the Loch Ness Monster as mysterious. I was left with my finger in the dike, a kinsman of those wooden shoe dancers at the Lynden Fair that I'd always made fun of.

But Kathleen eventually made lemonade out of that lemon. Using the LDS Church's huge genealogical database of the Middle Ages, she traced us back 26 generations, on one line, to Henry II (the first Plantagenet King of England) and therefore to his grandfather, William the Conqueror (Duke of Normandy). It seems that in 1830, we slipped in the back door when nobleperson Catherine Nicholson married a commoner, my great, great grandfather Abraham Rose. Good on you, Gramps.

Returning to London from Inverness by train, we shared a compartment with a charming and well-dressed elderly woman whose husband, we learned, was in the House of Lords. She had entertained us with stories about WWII for quite some time before she asked where we were staying in London. When Anne said, "The Marble Arch Marriott," the woman frowned, shook her head, and said, "How dreadful!"

Though certainly non-historic, and perhaps a bit plebian for aristocratic tastes, the Marble Arch Marriott was certainly fine for Bob and Anne. We popped up and got going each morning with a sumptuous buffet, including kippers, which made the Marble Arch M more than OK in my book. Thanks to London's great transportation system, we could rapidly get anywhere in the city on the Tube, or the double-deckers, so we saw everything that a good tourist should see. We even took a river-borne side-trip down the bustling, odoriferous Thames to the National Maritime Museum in Greenwich, so that this ancient mariner could step on the Prime Meridian longitudinal line.

Bussing ourselves over to Leicester Square each day, we bought half-price theatre tickets to some of the best shows of the time: *Phantom of the Opera*, *Les Miserables*, *Starlight Express,* and *Sunset Boulevard*. For pre-show dinners, we mostly avoided traditional English (boil until the taste is gone) cooking, and stuck to fish and chips or ethnic food in the West End theater district. That saved a lot of money (remember, we still thought we were Scots at the time).

A train change delay at Paddington Station provided one of our most memorable London moments. The owner of the Paddington Bear Store asked Anne to tend the shop while the lady went to the loo. You can imagine how excited that made my little bear collector. Anne sold three bears, if you include one to herself, before the woman returned and offered her a job. People like Anne.

We discovered cruising in 1999. Anne found a relatively cheap voyage leaving Vancouver for Alaska within three days. I told her that it didn't give me time to get any good boots for the Arctic tundra, but I agreed anyway. That first cruise exceeded my expectations; there were places to exercise, as much gourmet food as this gourmand could eat, Broadway production shows with beautiful women, great places to read my book while watching the ocean, and shore tours to do glaciers, narrow gauge railroads, and bear watching. I didn't once miss the hassle of checking in and out of hotels or looking for places to eat. And I didn't need those boots.

Three days into our second cruise to Alaska, Anne hurried to our table from the buffet line to tell us that some guy was talking about planes crashing into the World Trade Center buildings and the Pentagon. I said, "The security people should lock him up." But the ship's captain soon verified his story and we spent the rest of September, 11th, 2001, and much of the remaining cruise, glued to CNN, which was specially broadcast into various ship's spaces, including our staterooms. We all just wanted to get home, but even after we got off the ship that was no small feat: It took us hours to get through the U.S. border, only to emerge into a strange new paranoid world.

Because nobody wanted to travel after 9/11, Matt's United Airlines parent perks allowed us to fly standby and take advantage of extremely low cruise fares to

Alaska, Hawaii, the Panama Canal, and Europe. On planes one third full, United often flew us home business or first class, once from Amsterdam.

A repositioning (of the ship) cruise to Europe sure beat the old destroyer in the North Atlantic, but it attracted a lot of very senior citizens in varying states of dwindle and decay. In fact, all that fun was too much for at least four or five of them on that big ship, and they passed on. According to our dinner steward, their mortal remains were stored in the meat locker, so they'd keep till the end of the cruise. We couldn't help visualizing those poor, cold old folks down there alongside our soon to be eaten lobsters and filet mignons. Repositioning had a different meaning for them.

We safely toured Costa Rica's west coast on a Panama Canal cruise, but my luck ran out on a subsequent voyage when we floated a river on the Caribbean side. After watching birds, crocs, and monkeys for the better part of a morning, we stopped at a cruise-sanctioned jungle rest stop, where I hurriedly slaked my thirst with water from a water cooler. Then...Anne reminded me that we'd been previously warned to restrict ourselves to cokes and bananas. Oh, yeah....

Less than a week later, my punishment began. My gastroenterologist did a "million-dollar workup," concentrated on, but not limited to, the lower GI tract, but no cause was found. So I was given antibiotics, which helped not at all, and the condition was allowed to run its one-and-a-half-year Imodium slowed course.

On a follow-up visit, Barry, my eccentric GI doc (who wore his long hair and beard in Christ-like fashion) saw me and shouted, "ROSE, HAVE I GOT A STORY FOR YOU!" It seems that Barry's wife decided that they should vacation in Costa Rica for a change, rather than spend two January vacation weeks in Hawaii, as they usually did. Remembering my experience, he protested, but eventually gave in. Barry claims to have been extremely careful about what he drank, and how he drank it, but on his last day there he jumped in the swimming pool and involuntarily choked down "just a few drops of water—so help me God [funny coming from him]!" He had just completed *his* costly "no cause determined" workup and Imodium had become his best friend as well.

Next to Chelan, the Napili Sunset on the northwest coast of Maui is our favorite Vacation spot. We swim in Napili Bay, often near the Napili Kai, morning and afternoon, with or without flippers and snorkeling gear, in all kinds of weather, high and low surf conditions, never a problem—until there was.

After a ritual morning walk around Kapalua with Anne, I grabbed my snorkel and mask, sans flippers, and proceeded to check out the little reef fish hugging the coral reef remnants near the Napili Kai. After a bit, I noticed that it seemed harder to stay in position; in fact, I was starting to drift slowly seaward. Not to worry, swimming parallel to the beach would get me out of it, as it always had—but it didn't! "HEY, I NEED HELP HERE!" I shouted to some people watching from the Napili Kai, as I bobbed off the coral and drifted past their perch, somewhat faster now.

Soon, I heard a bullhorn bellowing at me, "RELAX, HELP IS ON THE WAY!" I was already on my back in deeper water, relaxing as much as one can in that situation. A surfer paddled out to me and we both climbed on his board and tried to paddle back to the beach, but we kept drifting out into Molokai Channel. "Hell, I've never seen it this bad," said my rescuer, "I easily paddled in a girl an hour ago."

Molokai seemed to be looming closer when we heard the buzz and slap of a wave-jumping jet ski—*the cavalry, at last!* Once I was clinging to its towed rescue board, the ski-doo zoomed in to the beach, where a large cheering and clapping audience was waiting, as were emergency medical vehicles. *How embarrassing!* It was incredible luck that I was swimming where I could be rescued, and that some shark a mile or two away hadn't smelled the blood I had oozing from small coral cuts on both my feet and come looking for a tasty meal.

Sudden heavy rain is not uncommon in Hawaii. Sometimes the red soil of the old Pineapple fields washes down into Napili Bay and turns it red, spoiling snorkeling for a day or two. But the most memorable deluge occurred while Anne and I were having dinner at Kapalua, a few blocks north of the Napili Sunset. As we were driving the short distance back to our condo, we saw water flowing over a dip in the road in front of us. My famous last words to Anne were, "It doesn't look very deep to me!" And I drove on. Suddenly, the car became a boat and we began floating toward a roadside drain abutment and the bay. Anne said, "I'm getting out of here," and opened the car door. Water started pouring into her compartment before she luckily got the door closed. Then a miracle: a black monster truck splashed up alongside and a big Hawaiian dude looked down from his driver side window and shouted, "HEH—I CAN PULL YOU OUT WITH A CHAIN, IF YOU DON'T CARE ABOUT THE BUMPER!" So he chained up, pulled us out, and towed us back to the condo, where he refused money. There are some really great people in this world.

Anne thought that a good retirement activity for me might be learning to dance properly. My parents were very good dancers, but in spite of considerable church and school dance exposure, my dance steps were a made-up medley. I did a lot of twirling and dipping to mask that fact. That was OK for most girls, but not Anne, a natural dancer, who'd been a guest dance instructor for the high school boys in Koosharem, Utah (population 300) and who was more recently a highly regarded international performer on the clogging circuit (Lynden, WA and White Rock, BC).

218

When Anne learned to kayak, I'd agreed to accompany her to a weekly dance class taught by a talented couple who'd built a ballroom above their garage. They thought that learning to dance should be fun, and indeed it was. I had to work hard, but was reasonably satisfied with my progress. On the last class night, our attractive female instructor asked me to dance with her...sort of a final exam, I guess. So I gave it my all. As the music ended and we came to a breathless stop, she whispered in my ear, "Bob, we'd be glad to let you take this class for another six weeks...for free."

I can't understand it. My Navy marching was OK, and that's a lot like dancing, isn't it? Fortunately, when granddaughter Kate and I danced at Brad's wedding, she didn't know that I'd flunked out of dance school, so we had a great time twirling and dipping...like in the old days.

Jazz ukulele (perhaps an oxymoron) seemed like a fun thing to take up in retirement. I had hoped to couple this with the fancy whistling techniques I'd used to fight off boredom while watering those seemingly endless Miller Floral rose beds. But I encountered a major problem: I couldn't play the ukulele and whistle at the same time, nor could I do either in front of an audience. Have you ever tried to whistle with people watching...and perhaps smiling? Unfortunately, my ukulele playing petered out, and my whistling soon did as well. Too bad. I'd always wondered how a CD of Bob Rose's all whistling version of the American Songbook would have been received if I'd stuffed one in everybody's stocking at Christmas?

Reminds me: I was caught whistling while on watch by a non-smiling Chief Petty Officer, on my first midshipman cruise. He vociferously informed me that there are only two kinds of people who whistle in the navy: *bosun's mates* (the tough sailors who "pipe" —with a whistle devise—the other sailors to their assigned tasks) *and damn fools.* "And, Midshipman Rose, *you sure ain't no bosun's mate!*"

LUMMI

L iving at Lane Spit was magical. The water was a living thing, usually swirling and lapping, but sometimes crashing and thundering, threatening to intrude upon us. There was a kaleidoscopic play of animal life: squawking seagulls, diving mergansers, drying cormorants, circling eagles, immobile herons, tiny bufflehead ducks, and tremolo calling loons. The heads of in-transit seals and otters occasionally bobbed to the surface, the otters sometimes bounding ashore to play around or under some vacant cabin. Deer passed by on their way to the water, sometimes bounding in to swim across the spit-narrowed, saltwater pass to reach the reservation. Seven herons were once seen fishing for candlefish in the bay, and thirteen eagles of varying ages converged to share a beach meal. We watched in wonder. And who could forget that lone coyote loping up the beach, stopping to stare at us—the Great Beach Spirit, we presumed.

The beach was the family gathering place for Christmas, Thanksgiving, most birthdays, and crab feeds, the grandkids sometime doing overnighters and weekenders. Because my sons married such great wives, they and their well-parented offspring were always welcome.

I occasionally got to minivan the grand-troops to and from the beach for sleepovers. In transit, we'd listen to CDs of their favorite musicals: Kate loved *The Sound of Music*, Spencer *The Music Man*, and Warren *Paint Your Wagon*. We eventually added *Camelot* and *My Fair Lady*, both of which we all saw together at the Mount Baker Theater. Gus wanted to hear *Hello Dolly*, because his favorite movie at the time, *WALL-E*, had some songs from that musical. Tori had no preference, I guess, but she was a baby so she couldn't tell us. You have to expose kids to "culture" wherever you can, even if you have to trap them in a car to do it.

Walks on the beach to see the crabs or "do the point (tip of Lane Spit)" began with Kate. At first, the tiny crabs we'd see scurrying away from the sheltering rocks we'd upended frightened her. She wouldn't touch them. But in time, she was not only picking up the little bi-clawed creatures, but searching for the smallest of those minute crustaceans she could find, white ones if possible. In cupped hands, she then started trapping the little slippery, thrashing eels she found at very low tides. These and other tidewater critters eventually became the purpose of our walks, which before long included her brothers, and eventually, Gus and Tori

In due course, both Spence and Warren conquered their DNA-engendered fear of holding creepy, crawly, and squiggly things in their hands, as Kate had. In fact, Spence holds the record for catching the largest hand-trapped eel. Warren was our chief anemone finder. He could see them even when they were camouflaged by seaweed, and would guide us around them like they were land mines.

Gus was an enigma. He seemed to have no fear of the beach's creepy crawlies from day one. He delighted in letting them inch over his hand for all to see and photograph. If Tori had been old enough, I think she would have handled the little creatures much like Gus did, and would have returned the little critters safely to their habitats, as we all did.

Kate loved to hunt for agates, colored glass pieces, and other artsy treasures on our beach walks, and she was good at it. She likes to hear my story about the perfectly round and shiny-smooth, five-millimeters, clear yellow-orange agate (the only such one I've ever seen) that she found when she was four years old. She insisted on carrying it around in her tightly closed fist, until she accidentally dropped the little gem between the deck boards when she opened her hand to peek at it. For years, she kept asking if we could tear up the deck to look for it.

Warren and Spencer each found at least one requisite agate, but they preferred to dam up a small stream gurgling down the beach or look for strange creatures in or near the surf: a giant red jelly fish, a dead shark, a live baby seal, or some creature that we'd never seen before and had to look up. Though everyone fished for bullheads, Warren had a passion for it at an early age. He and his friend Hayden made it a science, so my frozen crab bait larders were always full. I began paying a quarter a bullhead when I got to the beach (thought by old-timers to be exorbitant—rich doctor kind of stuff), so Warren and his friend cost me some real money, only limited by the available freezer space.

Kate made an art form of painstakingly searching for small rocks and shell fragments that she could glue-gun together to make many tiny animal sculptures. Spence glued up an attack clam and Warren a stone tank before they went out to bury each other in the sand for the hundredth time.

A crowd favorite was a boat ride to Seal Rock in "Old Yeller," our ancient yellow-hulled aluminum Duroboat, which was reliably propelled by a seemingly everlasting twenty-six-year-old, 9.9 horsepower Johnson motor. The twelve-foot-long craft would swoosh us along to Point Migley at breathtaking speeds, it seemed, while we looked for a wake to jump, even if it had to be our own. Every one of the older kids eventually learned to maneuver the boat, and Kate soloed in it before we left the beach.

We all loved "Wishing Rock Beach," as we called it, outings, a particular favorite of mine because I could get cheap labor to help me find and retrieve buckets full of superb glacier and surf smoothed rocks for my garden. A stop at the Islander for lollipops was my crew's reward. Another pricier trip to the store for Haagen-Dazs bars became an after-dinner routine, but that wasn't dependent on work.

Speaking of work, our beach sand was pristine and rock free because of the efforts of Warren and Spence, who sifted the sand through large screens each spring, before they buried themselves in it. Our neighbors asked us how we got our grandkids to work like that. It's simple: you pay them—well. And give them all the crab they can eat, of course.

Gus was still throwing rocks in the water, filling up trucks and cars with sand, and pushing his little scoot toy "downtown" when we left Lummi Island. He and Tori didn't get to bond with the beach as his older cousins had, which is unfortunate, but their family now has agate-scattered beaches and other Lummi-like features in the front and back of their cabin on Eliza Island. So that's a good thing. We'll be part of it when we can.

After we'd moved back to Bellingham, twelve-year-old Spencer observed, "You know Grandma, I had a better childhood because of Lummi."

LASTLY

In 1933, I won the birth lottery. I was born to loving, caring parents in a protective and encouraging mountain west society in the United States of America. My folks gave me good DNA and encouraged me to use at least some of the potential that gene-scramble created. Reasonably good public schools, a strong, motivating church, and a nurturing small community all contributed to my rearing, most of the time positively. I was lucky to get excellent higher education and my major career changes have, by and large, turned out well.

Good fortune put me out of harm's way for the major military conflicts of my time: I was too young for WWII (regretted by me then), in the NROTC for much of the Korean war, not re-activated for Vietnam (no blimp pilots needed), and way too old for the all-volunteer wars of Afghanistan and Iraq.

Exponential advances in technology have lengthened and enhanced my life. Without Microsoft Word, I probably wouldn't have written this history, which I've pecked out ever so slowly at twenty words a minute, enjoying every one of those minutes.

But best of all, I've now lived most of my life in one of the most beautiful places on earth. My lovely wife of fifty-three years, my three children, and my five grandchildren have enriched my life beyond measure. Thank you, Anne. I love you.

So, what's next? To paraphrase Alice Morse Earl: "Yesterday is history, tomorrow a mystery, and today a gift." I feel blessed to have been here in this time, place, and condition. It's been a good run.

ACKNOWLEDGEMENTS

I thank Bonnie Rose for the dynamic cover design, Anne Rose for helping me remember the kid's and grandkid's amusing behavior, and Sarah Rose for reading the manuscript. What a great family I have.

Additional thanks to Alyssa Quinn for her suggestions, Brendan Clark for the book design, and the staff at Village Books for their publishing expertise. We got it done.

CPSIA information can be obtained
at www.ICGtesting.com
Printed in the USA
LVHW070835240723
753240LV00014B/629